PENGUIN BOOKS

THE ART OF DECORATIVE STENCILING

Adele Bishop was educated at the Juilliard School of Music in New York City, the Ecole Normale de Musique in Paris, and the Accadèmia Chiggiana in Siena, and by private teachers in New York, Paris, and Rome. Remaining in Europe after her studies, she pursued a career as a singer and actress, appearing in both French and Italian films. In 1961, while living in East Hampton, Long Island, she became interested in stenciling, and two years later she and Cile Lord opened their custom stenciling studio in New York. Now living in Dorset, Vermont, she and her husband have formed American Decorative Arts, Inc., which supplies quality stencil kits and materials.

Born in Waco, Texas, Cile Lord studied at Baylor University, the Hoffman School, the Prang Textile Studios, and the University of Iowa, where she earned her master's degree in painting. She began stenciling professionally in 1963, when she and Adele Bishop founded their partnership, and today she operates her own studio in New York, designing and executing decorative work for private clients as well as teaching the art of stenciling. She also continues to paint, and her canvases have been exhibited in New York City and in East Hampton, where she now lives.

THE ART OF

DECORATIVE STENCILING

ADELE BISHOP

and

CILE LORD

PENGUIN BOOKS

Acknowledgments

Grateful acknowledgment is made for permission to reproduce color photographs of the authors' stenciling as follows: Plates 4 and 6, Patterson, Flynn & Martin; Plate of Roundtree Country Reproductions, Inc.; Plate 48 (photograph by Ernest Silva), courtesy *McCall's*, © 1974 The McCall Publishing Company. Plates 8 and 12 (© 1974, 1975 by Ernest Silva) and Plates 44 and 47 (© 1975 by Ernst Beadle) originally appeared in *McCall's*. Plates 45 and 46 were created for interiors by Hariet Eckstein.

Our thanks to *House & Garden* for Plate 17 (photograph by Horst, interior by Hariet Eckstein) and for the photographs on page 158. Plate 21 (photograph by Ernst Beadle, interior by Sue Morris), Plate 34 (photograph by Grigsby), Plate 37 (photograph by Ernst Beadle, interior by Goslee-Moore, Inc.), and Plate 40 (photograph by Ernst Beadle) are all courtesy *House & Garden*, © 1972, 1966, 1975, 1969 by The Condé Nast Publications, Inc.

Plate 39 (interior by Albert Hadley) and Plate 41 are courtesy *House Beautiful*, © 1970, 1971, by The Hearst Corporation. Other color and black-and-white photographs were made specially for the book by Don Gray and Edward Hardin.

We appreciate the courtesy of those who have provided photographs of historical examples: Plate 1, Mark Twain Memorial, Hartford, Connecticut; Plate 10, The American Museum in Britain, Bath, England; Plate 25, The Society for the Preservation of New England Antiquities.

NOTE

With the exception of the historical examples noted above, all the stenciling pictured in the book is by the authors. Plates 3, 7, 9, 11, 13–15, 16, 35, 36, 40, 42, 43, and 44 and Projects 1, 3, 6, and 7 are the work of Adele Bishop. Plates 2, 5, 8, 17, 19, 20, 21, 37, 38, 39, 41, 47, and 48 and Projects 2, 4, 5, and 8 were executed by Cile Lord. All other examples represent the combined efforts of both authors.

Penguin Books Ltd, Harmondsworth,
Middlesex, England
Penguin Books, 625 Madison Avenue,
New York, New York 10022, U.S.A.
Penguin Books Australia Ltd, Ringwood,
Victoria, Australia
Penguin Books Canada Limited, 2801 John Street,
Markham, Ontario, Canada L3R 1B4
Penguin Books (N.Z.) Ltd, 182–190 Wairau Road,
Auckland 10, New Zealand

First published in the United States of America by
The Viking Press 1976
Published in Penguin Books 1978
Reprinted 1981

LIBRARY OF CONGRESS CATALOGING IN PUBLICATION DATA
Bishop, Adele, 1927—
The art of decorative stenciling.
Bibliography: p. 195.
Includes index.
1. Stencil work.
I. Lord, Cile, 1927—   joint author.
II. Title.
[TT270.B57   1978]   745.7'3   77-28659
ISBN 0 14 00.4842 1

Printed in the United States of America by
Halliday Lithograph Corporation, West Hanover, Massachusetts
Color printed in Japan by Dai Nippon Printing Co., Ltd., Tokyo
Set in Linotype Bodoni Book

Contents

For Chips, Christian, and Claude
A.B.

For Jo Alys
C.L.

Preface

Our objective in writing this book is to share some of the joys and tremendous satisfaction we continue to experience each time we stencil—an enjoyment that must be attributed at least in part to the fact that we have been able to overcome some of the long-established limitations of stenciling.

Our progress has been extended by the discovery of clear acetate, a material that greatly expands design possibilities. Aside from the fact that it makes for a very durable stencil, this transparent material can be stacked in many layers over any design, and the elements of the design underneath may be traced in their entirety. In addition, we have worked out a reliable method of registering the stencils that results in perfect accuracy of application every time.

Concerned with perfect stenciling technique, we experimented with all types of paints and brushes. It was not enough to use just any stencil brush; we wanted a brush that would perform in such a way that the stenciling would be sure to have a quality of refinement. Equipped with the proper brushes and the technique to use them correctly, you can control qualities of shading that allow you to approximate various period styles.

You will also need to know what to stencil and what not to stencil, how to adapt a design and prepare it for stenciling. By trial and error, we gradually found the best and easiest ways to do everything possible connected with stenciling. The instructions in this book are the result of that practical experience.

Eight stenciling projects, arranged in order of increasing difficulty, are presented in Chapter 10. With each project, the systems for developing design progress. Once you understand how to interpret designs for stenciling and how to measure and mark off surfaces to be decorated, you will be able to apply this knowledge to any of your own projects. No working design is beyond the capabilities of the reader if the projects are studied in sequence. All the necessary general instructions are thoroughly covered in the chapters that precede the projects.

Chapter 11 is devoted to the theme of doing your own designing, with suggestions for finding and creating new designs and instructions for adapting, enlarging, and reducing them to suit your own purposes. For those who may not have the time or inclination to do their own designing, we have also included a collection of designs in a variety of styles. These may be copied, combined, or altered to fit any individual situation.

This book will teach you the art of stenciling with japan paint, but we hope it will accomplish much more as well. With a little imagination on your part, objects will come to life, and pattern and color will take on new dimensions.

1. The History of Stenciling

The history of stenciling is necessarily a history of fragments, bits and pieces found throughout both East and West, rarely more than a few examples to a century until relatively modern times. The origin of the process is unknown; quite possibly it was discovered in many different places at different times.

Some say that the Egyptians were the first to use stencils, as early as 2500 B.C., as decoration on mummy cases, though no proof of this has yet been found. Others contend that the Chinese originated the process even before 3000 B.C. In the Fiji Islands natives have traditionally used a stenciling process to add color and design to their clothing. There the irregular, angular cuts in the pattern are always similar, though never exactly the same. Anthropologists have theorized that the islanders adopted the shapes from the holes bored into bamboo and banana leaves by the larvae of a local insect.

Part of the problem in seeking the source—or sources—of the art derives from the perishable quality of the earliest stencils, which were probably made from leaves or soft pelts or skins. Not until the invention of paper in China, c. 105 A.D., was there any hope of one of these early stencils lasting through several centuries.

The earliest known stencil-like patterns come from the Caves of the Thousand Buddhas, at Tunhuang, in western China. Discovered by British Orientalist Sir Aurel Stein in 1907, the caves were located along once-flourishing trade routes between the Orient and the Middle East. Their contents date from between 500 and 1000 A.D. In one room were pieces of silk with the figure of Buddha outlined by stencil patterns, and the patterns themselves. The patterns were executed on a toughened, treated paper, with the designs outlined by thousands of tiny pinpricks. Charcoal was pounced through the

tiny openings to complete the transfer, and the outlines were then colored in by hand, so that these actually were not true examples of stenciling. Only when drawings are transferred directly, complete in both color and form, can they be considered stenciled in the full sense of the word, but the art from the caves provides an important link in stenciling's history.

The Chinese somewhat later invented a process called Derma printing, using an ink that incorporated the properties of an acid to cut a true stencil pattern. Wherever the ink was painted on paper, it ate through, leaving a clear-cut outline of the design.

As the art of stenciling blossomed in China and color and design were applied in one motion, its uses were at first limited to religious subjects. Before long more secular subjects, and artists, began to appear, and successful merchants became the stenciler's most important sponsors. A rich silk trade developed between China and its neighbors in the Orient, then was extended to the Middle East. By 600 A.D. intricate and colorful patterns stenciled on the fashionable materials worn by the wealthy had become the vogue. Somewhat later, stencils were used even on inexpensive cotton garments.

In Japan, India, Siam, and Persia the art of stenciling appears as early as 600 A.D., and it is in Japan that it probably achieved its greatest degree of refinement. There a unique artistic ability combined with a penchant for detail to produce some of the most beautiful stencil patterns ever seen. Unlike the Chinese, the Japanese were unhampered from the outset by any confinement to religious symbols. Instead they turned to nature for their subjects. Their stencils became detailed artistic studies.

The Japanese were aided in the production of sharp and intricate patterns by the discovery of a

Print made from an early Japanese stencil.

method for processing mulberry fiber into thin, rigid sheets by waterproofing the fiber with the juice of the persimmon. Previously old manuscript sheets had been used for stencils, but the mulberry sheets, once processed and dried, allowed for much cleaner and more detailed cutting. The design was cut on a hard surface, usually marble, with a knife held perpendicularly and directed away from the cutter. Once the cutting was completed, the sheet was covered with an adhesive or varnish called *shibu*, and single silk threads or individual human hairs were placed at quarter-of-an-inch intervals lengthwise and crosswise on the design to strengthen the patterns. Finally, a second cutout, exactly like the first and probably cut simultaneously, was placed over the varnished cutout to reinforce it further; the two were pressed, dried, and allowed to harden. The finished product was not only precise, it was also durable, and so expert and refined was much of the cutting that bridges between the cutout segments are often almost invisible.

The Siamese tended to dwell on the same subject matter as the Japanese. In remnants of stenciled fabrics found in Siam, flora and fauna provide the general ornamentation, but patterns are pinpricked rather than cut, for the most part. In India and Persia the technique was similar, but the subject matter differed. Persian artists turned to sacred stories for their inspiration, and Indian artisans devoted their attention to the endless possibilities of geometry—circle, square, and triangle—rendering them in as many variations as could be devised in search of the "perfect design." Some pastoral scenes also appear, but in nowhere near the profusion of the geometrics. Though such subject matter may not have been sacred, its inspiration was, for the Indian craftsman believed that only by doing as perfectly as possible the work for which he was destined could he advance spiritually.

The trade routes that carried the art of stenciling through the Orient carried it also into the West. It is believed that in Italy, early in the Christian era, stencils were used to teach children their letters. Many of the West's most notable leaders—Theodoric, king of the Ostrogoths; the Roman Emperor Justinian; Charlemagne—from the sixth century on used stenciled initials to sign their names to important documents. Most noteworthy from an artistic as well as historical point of view, however, is the stenciling found in France beginning in the Middle Ages, for there the art enjoyed widespread and varied use. In fact, the term "stencil" itself is derived from the Old French word *estenceler* (to sparkle) and the Latin *scintilla* (a spark).

And sparkle the decorations did—on playing cards, in books (where stencils were used to color illustrations reproduced by wood block), as wallpaper, and as ornamentation on textiles. Probably the broadest use of stencils occurred in the production of playing cards, produced in such volume that several edicts, both secular and nonsecular, were issued in an attempt to discourage their use. Eventually, in Italy, a tax was levied on the purchase of the cards. Unfortunately, however, few examples of either the early designs or the stencils still exist. Since the cards were made of paper, as they are today, they were usually short-lived, and inasmuch as one stencil was used again and again to produce the cards, the stencils, too, were destined to wear out all too soon, despite their relatively sturdy construction. However, many were later used to form the pasteboard backings in bookbindings.

In "Woodcut Stencils of Four Hundred Years Ago," in the *New York Public Library Bulletin*, Henry Meier tells of how he came across woodblock illustrations with stencil color in the binding of a book printed more than four hundred years ago. Erasmus's *Enchiridion Militis Christiani* was marked for rebinding at the library when Mr. Meier, examining it closely, discovered the tattered treasure—twenty-three bits and pieces of religious illustrations, as well as some fragments of stencil patterns from the late fifteenth and early sixteenth centuries. The specimens were as clean as if freshly cut and are recognized as the earliest preserved stencil designs of the period.

Despite the wide use of stenciling that is known to have existed in Europe, its development there as the meticulous art it had become in the Middle and Far East was slow indeed. Of the books printed during the fifteenth and early-sixteenth centuries in both Venice and Paris—the printing capitals of their respective countries—the stencil cutting was generally hasty and crude, and often so, too, was the wood-block workmanship. In surviving examples, such as the French *Histoire de l'Imagerie Populaire*, completed in the late 1400s, the stencil coloring is carelessly done, but in slightly later volumes, such as the *Cronica cronicarum abbrege et mis par figures, descentes et Rondeaulx*, printed in Paris in 1521, the craftsmanship is refined, indicating increasing care and attention to detail.

As Paris was the center for printing in France, Rouen became the center for the production of wallpaper, and as early as 1620 the names of individual artisans begin to appear as hallmarks. The first wall coverings were "flock papers," in which the pattern was sized on the paper with a stencil, and bits of shredded remnant wool were brushed onto the still-wet pattern to simulate brocade. Later the patterns were printed on the papers with wood blocks and then colored with stencils in the same way as book illustrations. Since the quality of the paper itself was poor, the wallpaper was never printed in rolls, but in segments called dominoes, approximately $12\frac{1}{2}'' \times 16\frac{1}{2}''$ in size. These expensive dominoes were used sparingly, often only as a decoration over a hearth or in a niche. In the earliest papers the designs of these segments were such that they could not be matched together to cover large areas.

Among the practitioners of this form of stenciling, Francis of Rouen was one of the first to make wallpaper in large volume and was well known for his fine craftsmanship. Les Bretons, father and son, produced marbled papers of excellent quality, often with gold and silver veining, and Sylvius von Benzennad was famous for his altar hangings. Most prominent of all, however, was Johann Claudius Renard, who boasted in the mid-eighteenth century that he could do anything with a stencil that could be done with a brush, and apparently made good his promise. So intricate were some of his designs that a number of stencils were often necessary to produce a single flower—roses were his specialty.

Stenciling in Europe seems to have achieved its high-water mark between the late-seventeenth and early-nineteenth centuries. In England and Germany stenciling appears on furniture, as wall ornaments in churches, and on wallpaper and textiles, though not as many examples of the art are still extant in either country, and its uses appear not to have been as widespread.

Just about the time that stenciling was reaching its greatest prominence in Europe, the settlers of North America began to enrich their lives with certain touches of refinement. Roughhewn houses with dirt floors and mud walls began to disappear. In an effort to imitate the carpeting of the Old World, simple painted decorations began to grace the wooden floors. First spatter painting was used, giving the floors a confetti-covered look, but soon more elaborate designs were sought. Repeated designs made possible through the use of stencils became border decorations surrounding a plain center, and eventually colors were mixed to produce greater diversity and aesthetic pleasure. Stenciled floors remained popular until almost the Civil War period.

Painting designs on floors was difficult. Most stenciled floors were the handwork of the "professional" decorator or house painter of the 1700s and 1800s, but floor cloths, a contemporary substitute for expensive carpeting, were produced by imaginative housewives as well as by the artisans of the day. The early cloths were imported from England, where they provided a durable, handsome, and inexpensive means of covering a not-too-attractive floor. Originally, most floor cloths were painted freehand on great pieces of canvas, sewed together, and stretched taut, but it was soon obvious that stenciling provided a quicker and more efficient means of producing repeated and intricate designs, although hand-painted versions continued to exist. Like the painted floors, the floor cloths boasted the advantage of designs that could be refurbished without too much cost or effort if the surface began to wear. Furthermore, canvas could be moved from one room to another if the owner fancied it, or taken along to new living quarters. George Washington in 1796 listed a floor cloth for $14.82 among his household expenses.

The stenciled patterns so useful for ornamenting floors and floor cloths were also employed as borders for plaster walls, which were becoming more and more common. Craftsmanship was not very expert at first—border patterns frequently did not meet symmetrically—but this too changed in time as skill improved.

For the most part, things common to the settlers' own existence were used in the patterns—flowers, leaves, stars, birds, bells, and the pineapple (which was a symbol of hospitality)—and they were repeated in stenciled designs on tin candle boxes and trays, on prized coverlets. These same forms sometimes appeared in the paintings on velvet (stenciled paintings called theorems) that adorned the walls of many American homes a century and more ago. By the early nineteenth century the most popular design was the American eagle, surrounded by stars equaling the number of states in the Union.

The patterns were completed by itinerant stencilers who roamed from town to town in search of such work, remaining in each place until all the work that could be contracted for had been completed. Their tools were simple—a few brushes, pigments, and some stencils. Most of this stenciling was done in coastal areas, not because the itinerant painters were unwilling to travel far inland, but because wallpapers had become more readily available. By the time the westward movement was fully under way, paper had begun to supplant paint as a form of wall decoration.

In addition, other types of American primitive art existed. One group of settlers—the Pennsylvania Dutch—brought with them from Europe a decorative tradition of their own. They were not Dutch at all, despite the designation, but Germans of various religious sects who settled in eastern Pennsylvania. Their work was characterized by well-balanced design, effective use of color, and little attention to perspective. A good deal of their work was done freehand at first, but stencils were eventually used to simplify repeated patterns, and the craftsmanship was almost always of the highest quality.

By the beginning of the nineteenth century in America the "homemade" was gradually being replaced by commercially produced furniture, the work of native sons or new emigrants. From the itinerant peddlers, stencilers, fix-it men, and early craftsmen of the 1700s, a generation of skilled workmen soon developed, ready to produce fine wares for general consumption.

Most prominent among such men was Lambert Hitchcock, who set up shop in the little town of Barkhamsted, Connecticut, in 1818. His pieces are easily identifiable, characterized by light, sturdy, straight construction. Most significantly, the pieces are painted, with painted (and later gilded) stenciling ornamenting the backs and legs. In addition, each of his chairs carried his name, transferred by stencil in yellow on the slat at the back—an early form of advertising and factory labeling.

Hitchcock was one of the first manufacturers to employ women. He hired them as stencilers, as did his contemporary Seth Thomas, one of the first large-scale producers of fine clocks in the United States. The women proved far more suited to the job than men, evidencing greater skill at rendering the sometimes intricate and delicate designs.

And there are other names that bear mention in American stenciling history: George Lord, the Eaton brothers, John Tallman, Francis Holland. These and others like them were instrumental in developing more and more detailed and intricate stencil patterns in this country, as the demand for such design moved from the large areas of floors and walls to chairs and clocks and finally to limited spaces on jewelry boxes, trays, and a score of other small household items.

Few American craftsmen have had so great an influence on decorative trends as Louis Comfort Tiffany, son of the wealthy founder of Tiffany, Young, and Ellis, which later became Tiffany and Company. Louis Tiffany began as a painter but soon found himself absorbed by his interest in commercial design, discovering new potentials in glass and interior decoration. His company, The Associated Artists, provided "artistic interiors" for the nation's prominent citizens, including President Chester A. Arthur during his brief stay in the White House, and Mark Twain, whose Hartford house he redecorated from top to bottom. Tiffany's love of opulence, bold forms, and vivid colors found expression in his handling of stained glass and in the use of stenciled borders, stenciled floors, and sometimes stenciling on entire walls and rooms. Unfortunately, the finest collection of Tiffany's work, which enjoyed popular approval from the late nineteenth century through the first three decades of the twentieth century, was housed in his own summer home on Long Island, which he had converted into an art foundation where aspiring artists might come as guests and study. When fire destroyed the building in 1957, important records of his work vanished forever.

Still, many of Tiffany's concepts, including his use of stenciled patterns, were repeated again and again in decorations in private homes and other buildings across the nation in the 1920s and 1930s, and the fads of the rich and notable were often used to a lesser extent by the middle class in planning the interiors of their homes. No house painter until the 1940s would have begun to work without his set of stencils for an intricate little border around the ceiling or along the top of each wall. These stencil patterns, however, were not always handled with the best of taste or designed to permit careful execution. The fact that the stencils themselves were commercially produced by the thousands and could be bought for a pittance usually did not add to their aesthetic possibilities.

By World War II plainer and simpler interiors had become the vogue, and the precious qualities of a stenciled border along floor or wall were no longer in demand. Not until almost twenty years later did widespread interest reappear. As is always true, a few dedicated artisans have led the way, their interest and enthusiasm extending the craft to new artistic dimensions.

We are proud to have contributed improvements in methods that make stenciling far more accessible than before to the amateur craftsman. Although we have only begun our exploration of these simplified techniques, we have been able to elaborate the art far beyond its traditional limitations.

So effective is the art, so broad are its applications, and so adaptable is its form, that it is not surprising that it has endured so well.

2. Stenciling Today

Although stenciling was used by primitive peoples as one of the earliest decorative forms, the importance of its role has varied for hundreds of years. With each revival of its popularity stenciling has reached another peak only when it was called upon to fulfill a particular need. Today stenciling is the answer to the problems of those who are aware of a great void in decoration that cannot be filled by commercially—and synthetically—produced effects. In its present revival the craft is being enjoyed not by modern antiquarians, expert craftsmen, or collectors, but by people much the same as the artisans who stenciled walls and floors in their homes 150 to 200 years ago. They are people who want some form of decoration in their homes and find it infinitely more appealing when it is hand-done, expressed in their own terms, and in their own choice of design.

Stenciling is any method of decorating that involves using a brush or other implement to apply color through shapes cut out of a sheet of impervious material. It is not our aim here to explore the entire realm of the craft, but we do need to define two accepted methods—bronze powder and japan paint stenciling.

Bronze powder stenciling is done with finely ground metallic powders, such as bronze, aluminum, and even gold and silver. The powders are applied by rubbing them through the openings in the stencils onto a varnished surface that is tacky enough for them to adhere to it. A black or very dark background must always be used to create the illusion of depth characteristic of this style of stenciling, making the range of color possibilities quite limited.

Japan paint stenciling is done with instant-drying paints composed of pigments ground in a japan medium. The paint is applied with a stencil brush to fill in the cutout shapes in the stencil. The japan colors may be applied over a background of any color.

With few technical limitations, the range of stenciling possibilities provided by japan paints becomes fantastic. It is not difficult to see why this method is the choice of the present stenciling revival and why we have chosen it for emphasis here. With its crisp, precise look, japan paint stenciling reflects a style appealing to nearly all of us today.

One could claim that any stenciled design could just as easily be hand-painted. However, while it takes longer to prepare and cut stencils, the time involved in executing the actual design is shortened immeasurably, especially when it is to be repeated many times over a large surface or on several surfaces. One must also bear in mind that to paint a design freehand, it must first usually be drawn accurately onto the surface. You need never do this in stenciling. Nor do you have to master a style of brushstrokes, such as those used in the execution of tole painting or rosemaling.

What then is the special allure of stenciling? Why does it appeal to more and more people every day? Certainly the time element has given stenciling some of its universal appeal, but decorating today is concerned with a personal visual experience. Its inclination is not to conform exclusively to period styles of decor but to convey individual impressions and sensations. Stenciling offers everyone great freedom in bringing about this experience. It is not restricted to black backgrounds and metallic colors, or to specific surfaces or objects. You do not have to master brushstrokes and spend long hours hand-painting every shape. There are no set rules to conform to other than your own taste and your own feelings and ideas. Once you have acquired the technical know-how, you will be in a position to cause these ideas to take form.

Just about any piece of wooden furniture can be stenciled, although there are exceptions. Some objects have a generous amount of carved ornamentation and should be left alone. Others may have lines so pure and simple and an existing finish so handsome that it would be a shame to change them. Rounded surfaces, such as curved legs, rails, and spindles, also must be avoided, because the stencil must lie on a more or less flat surface to discourage paint from running under it.

Wooden floors, however, can be beautiful when stenciled. It doesn't really matter whether or not they are in good condition, are parquet or regular floor boards. The design will conceal any flaws in the wood, and stenciling is often the solution for problem floors. Barn floors or plywood subfloors may be covered with hard-finish masonite cut into tile-like squares in dimensions convenient for application. This inexpensive and practical way of creating a "new" floor makes it possible to do the painting and stenciling on a table and then set the masonite tiles down later.

Asphalt or vinyl tile and linoleum cannot be stenciled. Their slick, waxlike surfaces prevent paint from adhering properly and eventually cause it to chip.

It is difficult to imagine the great charm of a stenciled wall without ever having seen one, or at least having seen good photographs of some of the old stenciled walls to be found throughout New England. Many people feel it is too much of a bother to stencil walls when wallpapers are easily available, but a stenciled wall will always have a quality that no wallpaper can ever achieve. The stencil artist is completely free to interpret in different ways the intervals of space brought about by the windows and doors in a room. Windows and doors can be framed with delicate borders. Paneling effects can be produced. One can keep the design simple and elegant with merely a frieze running along the top of the ceiling or a border running above a dado. A more ornate look can be achieved by combining all-over designs with borders. Fireplace mantels can be incorporated into the surrounding design. Wall sconces can be embellished with lovely encircling borders. Many more individual things can be accomplished with stencils than can ever be done with wallpaper.

In the past, stenciling was always done directly on plaster walls. Today most houses are lined with plasterboard. When a flat, opaque paint is applied to plasterboard with a roller, the result is nearly the same as that of plaster. Stenciling has been done on painted wood paneling and can certainly be done on contemporary veneer paneling. Old wallpaper can be painted over and then stenciled. Cloth-covered or fiber-covered walls are handsome when stenciled, because a bit of texture in the background always makes a design more interesting. Unlike floors and furniture, stenciled walls do not need a protective coat of varnish. Soiled spots can be washed off with mild soap and warm water after the paint has set for six months and has become well seasoned, with all the vapors completely evaporated.

There is no limit to the many ways stenciling can be used throughout the house, in making gifts for family and friends, and as a commercial venture. You must let your imagination run free and remember that there are few technical limitations to stand in your way. Some of the many objects that might be stenciled are: beams, book covers, boxes, baskets, mailboxes, wastebaskets, pillows, draperies, doors, shutters, signs, wood dishes, cabinets, chairs, floors, fabric, canvas or grass mat rugs. Also flowerpots, leather, window shades, frames, garbage cans, fireplace mantels, old-fashioned milk cans, stepladders, moldings, stools, sconces, stair risers, screens, tables, table mats, tinware, old-fashioned bathtubs, trunks, trays, wooden toys, and just about anything else that offers a paintable surface.

Today there are many more materials suitable for stenciling than our ancestors could have imagined. Modern synthetic materials imitate fibers that would be prohibitively expensive to buy now. The only rule to adhere to when confronted with the problem of selecting materials is to avoid slippery surfaces, including glass, high-gloss finishes, porcelain bathroom fixtures, ceramic tile. Don't try to stencil on surfaces treated with any form of wax or glossy finish that resists paint. Textured materials are usually quite effective when stenciled, but a delicate design composed of very small shapes is unsuitable on a rough texture. Worth considering are brick, concrete, stone, terra cotta, sheetrock, masonite, composition board, barn siding, cloth, paper, leather, canvas, straw matting, plywood, burlap, parchment, plaster, wood, and textured synthetics.

When you are ready for your first project, be sure to select a design you can handle with ease so that you will maintain confidence and enthusiasm.

Stenciling with japan paints is a very rapid way of applying design, but never cut your work schedule so short that you find yourself rushed and frenzied. In a relaxed mood, you can easily maintain a standard of excellence. Remember, stenciling offers not only very rewarding results—it is therapeutic and fun!

Examples of the authors' stenciled designs.

14

3. Materials and Equipment

If you know exactly what to expect from all your stenciling materials and tools before you start, you will progress much more rapidly as a stenciler. Study your equipment beforehand and you will achieve far more satisfying results than if you attempted to resolve problems by trial and error.

The individual properties and uses of the basic materials needed for japan paint stenciling are explained below. The list of Supply Sources at the end of the book tells where you can buy materials if they are not available locally.

Stencil Materials

Clear acetate in .0075 gauge is ideal for stencils. Anything thinner will tear; anything heavier will be too difficult to cut. Buy acetate in flat sheets rather than by the yard from a roll; acetate is very difficult to straighten once it has been curled up. Clear acetate is completely transparent, cleans easily, and outlasts any other stencil material. It takes longer to cut than other stencil materials, but its transparency makes the entire tracing and stenciling procedure go faster.

Frosted Mylar, bought in sheets, may be used with either japan or acrylic paint. For stencils, .005 gauge is best. Although it is not entirely transparent, designs can be seen and traced through three or four layers of Mylar. The frosted kind takes both pen and pencil marks well, and the stencils may be bent or folded easily to fit into difficult corners or other spaces. Almost as easy to cut as stencil paper, Mylar is far more durable. Its cost is similar to that of acetate. Be sure to get *frosted* Mylar.

Vinyl. Clear 8-gauge vinyl can be purchased by the foot or yard from rolls 54″ wide. Inexpensive and easy to cut, this plastic material can be used with either acrylic or japan paints, but is too stretchy for stencil shapes which must be traced, cut, and painted with fine accuracy. Vinyl has a tendency to ripple, does not hold ink, and rejects pencil lines completely.

Morilla stencil paper is the best choice for paper stencils. Like Mylar, it is translucent, not transparent, and so is best suited for simple designs that are easy to trace. Morilla stencil paper is easy to cut. Tracing may be done in pencil. (The Morilla Company distributes more than one kind of stencil material under its own name; be sure to get the stencil paper that has been treated by a dry-wax process, and not the opaque or the heavily waxed kind.) All paper stencils are relatively fragile and do not last well under repeated use. Paint cannot be completely removed from them.

Oaktag (stencil board). A heavy paper stock used for file folders and commercial letter stencils, oaktag is opaque. Easy to cut out, easy to locate, and inexpensive, this material can be used successfully for some simple types of stenciling.

Waxed stencil paper is sold by the sheet. It has a heavy coating of wax on both sides and is translucent. Neither pencil nor pen can be used to trace the design onto it, and the wax may rub off onto the stenciling surface or into the paint.

Architect's linen, sometimes used for bronze paint stenciling, should *not* be used to make stencils for use with japan paint. The friction of the brush stretches this material so that paint runs under the stencil.

Stencil Brushes

The ideal brush is not necessarily the one sold as a stencil brush. Two types of brushes excellently adapted to stenciling are a *cabinetmaker's gluing brush* and a *rubbing brush*. Both of these brushes are made of a bristle far superior to that of the ordinary stencil brush. A very large brush works just as well as a smaller one and will cover a large surface area in very little time. The bristles are flexible enough to permit beautiful shading. Both these brushes are more expensive than conventional stencil brushes and may be difficult to locate, but they are worth every effort to obtain them. It is essential to have a separate brush for each color.

Drawing Tools and Equipment

A technical drawing pen, such as the Koh-i-noor Rapidograph or Castell TG pen, should be used to trace designs onto acetate. Designed for use with India ink, it has a continuous ink flow. Points come in several thicknesses, but the best sizes for the stenciler are #00, #0, or #1. Use regular black India ink or Koh-i-noor Rapidograph ink. All register marks needed on the stencil are made with this pen, because the ink, when dried, resists wearing off. A conventional pen staff and pen point and

Brushes. The short brushes are known as rubbing brushes. The long-handled brush is called a gluing brush. All are used for stenciling.

Stenciling equipment. Top: Technical marking pen, plumb line, and masking tape. Center: Palette knife with offset handle. Bottom: Utility knife.

India ink will do for tracing designs onto Mylar or acetate, but changes of pressure vary the line, making tracing less accurate. Drawing straight lines with a ruler and an ordinary pen nib is impossible; the ink usually runs under the ruler.

Pencils, well-sharpened, are sufficient for tracing designs onto Mylar or paper stencils and are needed for drawing designs and for measuring and marking stenciling surfaces.

Drawing board—essential for drawing and tracing designs. One with a metal edge makes measuring more accurate. A practical size is 18″ × 24″.

T square and right-angle triangle—these draftsmen's tools help to establish straight lines and perfect right angles.

Cross-section paper (graph paper) is helpful for planning repeat patterns and for enlarging and reducing designs. A grid of eight squares to the inch is most versatile. Working out repeats on paper saves a lot of measuring.

Compass—necessary for drawing perfect circles.

Tracing and drawing paper in pads of small- and medium-size sheets are adequate for most design needs.

Metal ruler—an 18″ size is best for general use.

Cutting Tools

The **utility or mat knife**, Stanley Model #299, is ideal for cutting all stencil materials. The cutting blade must be changed as often as needed to do a good cutting job. Always use the Stanley knife blade #1991–5; do not buy heavy-duty blades. For cutting Mylar or paper stencils, the Stanley utility knife or an X-Acto knife, Model #11 or #16, will do. The X-Acto knife is not sturdy enough to cut acetate.

Stencil Paints and Solvents

Stencil paint must be instant-drying if it is to be used effectively. Paint that dries slowly runs under the stencil while it is being applied and smudges when the stencil is moved.

Japan colors (also known as japan paints or signwriter's japan colors) are pigments ground in a quick-drying, resinous varnish which contains little or no oil. Flat and opaque, they dry instantly. The solvent is turpentine. Japan colors can be purchased in tubes or in 8-ounce (½ pint) cans. (In the directions in this book, a "tube" refers to the 37 cc or 1.25 fluid ounce size.) If not readily located in stores, japan colors may easily be ordered by mail. The japan colors used for stenciling should not be confused with the kind of quick-drying enamels that are sometimes sold as "japan paints." Made in a limited range of colors for painting cast metal, these enamels are not adequate for decorative stenciling.

Acrylic paint, available in jars or tubes in a wide variety of colors, is water soluble but forms a tough, hard-to-remove skin on both stencil and brush. Although satisfactory for use with vinyl or Mylar, acrylic paint should not be used with stencils of acetate or paper. The acrylic medium curls the acetate; the water used to thin it gradually dissolves paper stencils. It also washes off ink registration marks, so that the stencils can be registered only with notches. Acrylic paint may be used to tint acrylic gesso or water-base paints employed in painting backgrounds.

Artists' oil paints may be used in very small amounts to tint japan colors, but only when absolutely necessary, because the oil content slows down the drying process. Glazes can be tinted with artists' oils. Turpentine is the solvent.

Textile paint. Stenciling on fabrics requires specially prepared textile paints, such as Prang. The manufacturer provides full directions for use. Also widely available is Flo-Paque.

Turpentine. Gum turpentine is best for thinning the japan or oil paint and cleaning stencils, and for making glazes or mixtures for antiquing backgrounds.

Mineral spirits (paint thinner) is needed for cleaning brushes and may be used to thin background paints. Do *not* mix it with japan paint.

Essential Miscellanea

Masking tape is used in a 1″ width for taping down and hinging stencils and for masking out design areas that are to be left unpainted. A ¾″ width might be substituted.

Transparent tape is essential for repairing stencils. "Magic"-type Scotch tape, which appears frosted but becomes transparent when applied, is less brittle than the clear kind.

A small glass bowl holds turpentine for cleaning stencils and thinning stencil paint.

Facial tissues and **paper towels** have many vital uses. Buy plain white ones in a sturdy quality.

Teaspoons are used for measuring and mixing turpentine with paint.

Palette knife (offset trowel type) is used for mixing stencil paint.

Saucers, preferably white, are used for mixing paint. Always use a separate one for each color. White saucers make it easier to judge color tones.

Piece of plate glass is useful for cutting stencils and occasionally for mixing colors. A good size is 10″ × 12″ and ¼″ thick. Have the corners and edges filed smooth. Paint the underside of the glass white or slip a piece of white paper under the glass for better visibility.

Kneaded eraser is good for erasing pencil and chalk marks and correcting small stenciling errors.

Proof paper consists of brown wrapping paper or any large sheet of smooth paper suitable for making proofs.

Paper buckets or **empty coffee cans** are useful for holding and mixing large amounts of stencil paint that are to be applied with a roller.

Yardstick and/or a **tape measure** is needed for measuring and marking off large surfaces.

Backgrounds and Finishes

The following materials may be used for preparing the surface before stenciling and for finishing it afterward:

Acrylic gesso, a pure white water-base material which comes ready-mixed in cans and jars, is often used by artists to prime canvas. White or tinted, it is employed by the stenciler only for preparing the surface to be stenciled, never for the stenciling process itself.

Wood stains—to prepare plain wood surfaces for stenciling, buy ready-mixed wood stains, or use a natural-color oil-base sealer and tint it with japan color or universal colorants.

Varnish—there are three varnish finishes: flat, satin (semigloss), and gloss. Varnish is used for mixing glazes and as a protective coating before or after stenciling. Select one that is water- and alcohol-proof. Polyurethane varnishes provide a very durable finish and are often recommended for floors. Varnish is usually applied with a brush but can be put on with a roller. Its slight beige or amber cast becomes more pronounced with consecutive applications.

Spray varnish and spray shellac are occasionally useful as fixatives to protect small areas of stenciling from bleeding or running during finishing.

Clear shellac has an important function as a wood sealer or as a protective coat to isolate any stenciling that shows a tendency to bleed or dissolve under brush varnishing. Its solvent is denatured alcohol.

Denatured alcohol—for thinning or dissolving shellac.

Universal colorant—concentrated pigment purchased in tubes for tinting both water- and oil-base paints.

Rottenstone—this common rubbing compound is mixed with wax for antiquing purposes.

Butcher's Wax (clear)—hard, carnauba-base wood-finishing paste wax. For final finishing or, mixed with rottenstone, for antiquing.

Tack cloth—specially prepared cloth for picking up dust particles before varnishing.

Metal primer—oil-base paint made especially to help prevent rust on tin and ironware. Usually comes in black or orange. Several brands are available.

"Rusticide"—liquid preparation used to clean off rust and help prevent further rusting.

Wall and floor paints—for applying backgrounds. Always buy a flat (matte) paint or satin finish for backgrounds, never gloss paints or enamels.

Paintbrushes—use nylon brushes for applying gesso, and nylon or natural bristles for applying paint. Follow recommendations on the paint can. For varnishing, use a special varnish brush and do not use it for anything else.

White primer (such as B-I-N)—a specially prepared shellac-base primer to which white pigment has been added. Primer seals wood and prevents knothole bleeding.

Production paper (sandpaper)—for sanding wood and gesso, medium (#80) and fine (#120) production paper are needed.

Steel wool serves to smooth out bumpy dust particles imprisoned by the varnish as it dries, and to burnish waxed surfaces. It is also handy for wearing down a stencil print to produce a worn or antique look. Use either fine (#000) or very fine (#0000).

Note: The ingredients in strong cleaning preparations and in solvents, paints, varnish, and shellac (particularly those in spray cans) may be toxic. Always work in a well-ventilated room and carefully observe the manufacturers' warnings on labels.

Equipment for Large Projects

Decorating large surface areas such as walls and floors calls for a few items of special equipment not ordinarily needed in stenciling:

Plumb line (chalk box)—for marking off large areas for repeat designs. A metal box houses a string (the plumb line) which can be pulled out to various lengths. Blue or white chalk within the box coats the string. When the string is pulled out and snapped, it leaves a perfectly straight chalk line on the decorating surface. This device is invaluable for placing a grid of straight lines over the extent of a floor or wall, or establishing lines for borders over large areas.

Paint rollers—for stenciling large geometric designs and designs with exceptionally large shapes, or painting plain backgrounds. Purchase a plush mohair roller with a standard handle, in either a 4″ or 7″ size.

Roller pans—for roller stenciling.

Cookie sheets—to hold paper towels for roller stenciling and to serve as trays to hold stencil materials.

A traditional stencil design.

4. Preparing the Stencil

Traditional stencil design

Traditional stencil design in America is easy to recognize. The presence of intervals between the cutouts gives these painted decorations a recognizably "stenciled" look. The intervals not only serve as bridges between the openings in the stencil but function as an important part of the design itself.

The transparent stencil

The intricate design at right does not look stenciled. However, it was applied with six stencils, using one after another. Today more complicated designs can be printed without intervals by using transparent plastic stencils. The transparency makes it possible to divide and trace a design onto several layers of the stencil material stacked over each other. Because you can see through the stencils, they can be aligned perfectly by a system of ink-mark registration that allows you to re-create almost any example of design regardless of its complexity. The plastic stencil will not deteriorate or wear out. After a simple cleaning it is as good as new.

Choosing materials

The term "plastic" covers a wide range of synthetic materials all derived from similar sources. By adding various solvents, the manufacturer obtains different products. Acetate, Mylar (polyester), and vinyl all share the common virtue of being transparent or translucent, and surpass all other stencil materials for durability. However, because vinyl does not hold the ink marks so essential to an effective registration system, acetate and Mylar are more satisfactory as stencil materials.

Design printed from transparent stencils.

Single stencil design.

The cutout stencil.

Acetate is completely transparent, so an unlimited number of sheets may be superimposed to extract and trace quickly and easily the elements of a design onto successive stencils, and the registration marks may be made at the same time. Rigid and sturdy, it holds India ink marks well. Unlike vinyl, it will not ripple and cause inaccuracies in registration and printing.

The translucency of frosted Mylar limits the stenciler to superimposing no more than four stencils to trace the designs and make the necessary registration marks. Consequently intricate designs requiring many stencils cannot be reproduced easily with Mylar. Paper stencils, being both fragile and less translucent, obviously have very restricted functions in decorative stenciling, although they sometimes serve well as a supplement to plastic stencils in special situations.

Which stencil material you choose to work with will depend upon your own needs and inclinations, but for our own purposes we have found that acetate allows a degree of versatility in design that is not possible with anything else. The designs in this book, with rare exceptions, have all been executed with acetate stencils and japan paint, but instructions are given later in this chapter for cutting and registering stencils of other materials as well.

Setting up work
Choose a place with the best lighting possible. Make sure the surface you do your tracing on is smooth and hard. A drawing board is ideal. You will want enough space for a piece of glass at least 10″ × 12″ and plenty of elbowroom besides. Use a technical drawing pen and India ink for tracing designs onto acetate. Always wash your hands before working with acetate; any smudges of oil from your fingers will keep ink from properly adhering to the surface. If you are using Mylar, you may trace the design with a pencil, but placement and registration marks should be made in ink, as they must be permanent.

If the stencil material has a slight curve, place the material so that it curves down as you trace the design.

The single stencil design
A single stencil is usually printed in only one color. The bridges between the cutout shapes are an important part of the design. To trace the design for stenciling, begin with a piece of stencil material large enough so that it will leave a 1″ margin all around the outside of the entire design. This margin keeps the brush from smudging over the edge of the design in stenciling. Tape the stencil material over the design with masking tape to secure it in place. You are now ready to trace the designs above and below and cut the stencils.

Cutting a stencil.

Cutting the stencil

To cut out shapes in an acetate stencil, use a utility knife. Keep the blade sharp. Each blade has two points. If the knife begins to slip and cutting becomes hard to control, your blade probably needs to be changed. For Mylar, use either a utility knife or an X-Acto knife. Never work with a dull blade.

Lay the traced stencil down on a piece of glass that is backed with white paint or paper so you can see what you are doing. Begin cutting anywhere in the design. Hold your knife exactly as you would hold a pencil. The fingers of your other hand should rest firmly on the stencil at all times, turning it slowly so that you are always cutting toward you.

In order to achieve a smooth line, practice lifting your cutting blade from the stencil as little as possible. *Remember to keep turning the stencil so you are always cutting toward you.* Make full use of your cutting arm, wrist, and hand in a completely co-ordinated and natural movement. Your arm will tire at first, but with practice you will become stronger, able to cut stencils for hours with a minimum of fatigue.

Your blade must always be *directly on the traced line,* not outside or inside it. When all the shapes have been cut out, hold your stencil up to the light and examine it. Look for jagged contours, overcutting (cutting beyond the end of the line), or cutting inside or outside the lines. The bridge between the cutouts must be wide enough to be able to withstand constant going over with the stencil brush and repeated cleanings after use. Too delicate a bridge will break. Practice cutting until you are pleased with the shapes produced.

When you have cut out a satisfactory stencil, you are ready to make a trial proof of the design. With a moistened tissue remove any traces of ink left around the cutout shapes. Select a color that will show up well, and following the basic directions in the next chapter, make proofs on your paper until they are technically perfect. Practice tracing and cutting the design below and those on pages 24 and 25.

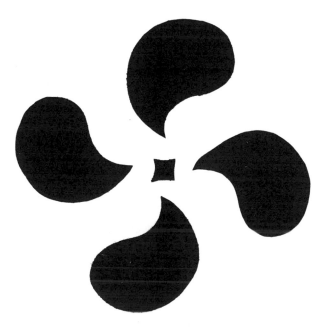

Multiple stencils

Using more than one stencil in a single design enables you to print more than one color, to eliminate the bridges in the design, and to divide into sturdier sections a vulnerable shape that might otherwise tear or break.

Learn how to divide elements of a design onto different stencils. To demonstrate how this is done, we have taken a simple Early American flower design as an example. A different tone of gray is used for each color that is to be put on a separate stencil. To print this typical traditional design in two colors, two stencils will be necessary, one for each color.

Cut two pieces of stencil material, each large enough to allow a 1″ margin around the outside of the design. Tape one of the pieces over the complete design, A, but trace only the parts of the design shown in B. Leave the stencil on the design. Place the second piece of stencil material over it. Tape it securely. Trace the parts of the design shown in C. Before removing the tape, make the register marks as described below, indicate the "Top" on each of the stencils, and number them.

Register marks

In order to print two stencils in proper relation to each other, you will need to make register marks on the second stencil as shown in C. The register marks follow precisely the contours of the shapes in the first stencil. Use a broken line for these marks so they will not later be mistaken for cutting lines. Although such a simple design could be placed by eye, a more complex design relies on very accurate placement, so you should learn to use register marks at the outset.

A =

Each of the designs at right uses two stencils. The colors are indicated by different tones to show which shapes go on each stencil. Practice tracing these designs onto two separate stencils and make the register marks as shown in the illustrations above.

Top 1.

Top 2.

B   +   C

Design requiring three stencils.

Stencil 1.

If the design calls for three stencils, the register marks will appear only on Stencils 2 and 3.

Always make the register marks on subsequent stencils by following the shapes printed from the *first* stencil. To be sure your register marks are accurate, place each succeeding stencil over the proof taken from the *first* stencil and make sure the register marks follow its printed contours exactly. Erase with a moistened tissue any that are incorrect and redraw them.

Stencil 2. Register marks are taken from a *print* of Stencil 1.

Stencil 3. Also takes register marks from a print of Stencil 1.

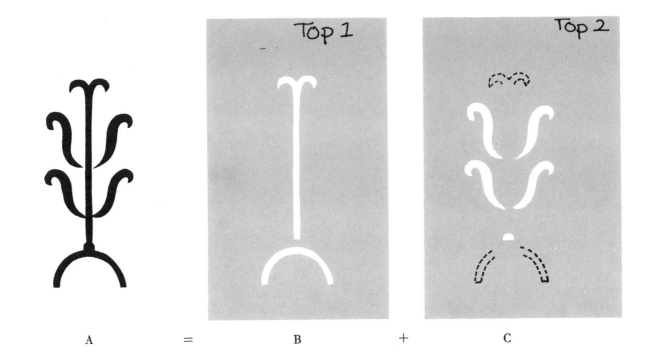

A = B + C

Eliminating the bridge

A design that is to have no bridges between the shapes requires two stencils even though it may be printed in only one color. You can see above the need for precise register marks to prevent over-lapping or gapping.

These designs have two things in common: they do not include bridges as part of the design, and they could not have been made with only one stencil.

Stencils for multicolor designs

Executing designs in more than two colors is simply a matter of using more stencils. Each color takes usually one stencil. By using an extra stencil you can do away with the bridge between cutout areas. The designs shown here illustrate this. They are printed in two or more colors and show no bridges. Practice dividing the design onto the necessary stencils. Use separate stencils for each color and to eliminate bridges between shapes. More than one color may be printed with one stencil provided the cutout areas are far enough apart so there is no danger of the brush accidentally printing the wrong shape. For printing more than one tone of a single color, the same procedures may be used.

Although the flowers in the design above are to be printed in different colors, they may safely be traced and cut in a single stencil because they are widely spaced, as shown below.

Dividing vulnerable forms

Some designs, if cut in only one stencil, produce shapes that will cause the stencil to break easily during stenciling or cleaning. Such designs should be divided onto two stencils. Select a division that allows for a sturdy bridge between the separate shapes.

The following figures illustrate the right and wrong ways to do this:

Right: A = B + C

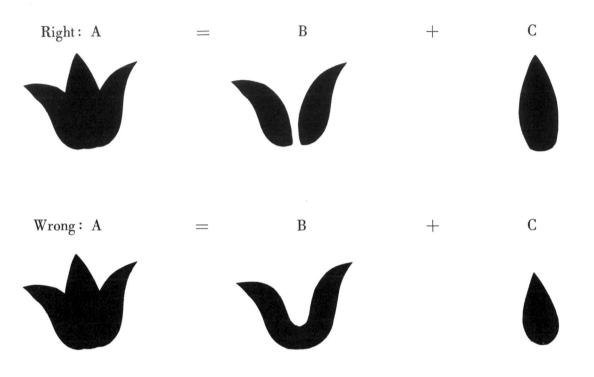

Wrong: A = B + C

Here is another problem shape with a good solution, using two stencils:

A = B + C

32

Removing ink from acetate or Mylar

India ink is water-soluble. Any unnecessary ink marks may easily be wiped off acetate with a slightly moistened tissue. Never immerse acetate in water; it will curl up.

Cleaning a clogged pen

A technical drawing pen may clog up when not in use, and dried ink is difficult to dissolve. Thoroughly wash the pen with warm water after each use. Rinse until no trace of ink is left. If you must put your work aside until the next day, or even for only two or three hours, immerse the lower half of the pen in a glass of water. This will prevent any clogging of the delicate tip of the pen and will keep it functioning properly.

Repairing stencils

When a stencil tears (usually on one of the stencil bridges), the broken section frequently is still partially attached. Stick small pieces of transparent tape to both sides of the stencil, being sure the damaged piece is correctly placed. Trim away any excess tape. If your blade slips and overcuts a shape, repair the stencil in the same way.

When a piece has actually been broken off from the rest of the stencil, you will have to perform a little plastic surgery. Trace the shape of the broken-off piece onto a small piece of stencil material. If the piece is lost, trace from the original print. Cut out the replacement with a utility knife and tape it in place, taping both sides of the stencil. Trim away any excess. This is rather meticulous work, especially if the piece to be repaired is very small. Have patience, do the work carefully, and your stencil will be as good as new.

Gapping

Gaps in printing may be caused by stencil shapes that are cut too small. Correct such miscutting immediately. Make a proof of the design and place the stencil over it. Where an unintentional gap appears on the proof, correct it on the stencil with the marking pen, then trim it to the proper size.

Stencil care

When you have finished stenciling, clean the stencils and put them away in good condition. Don't allow them to pile up or lie scattered about. Stencils should be thoroughly cleaned and examined for breaks, tears, or weak sections before storing. An organized collection of well-cared-for stencils promotes fine craftsmanship.

Instant identification of designs is important if you are building up a large collection of them. It is hard to visualize a finished design by looking at a transparent stencil full of holes, and you won't want to go to the trouble of making proof prints each time to find the right design. Keep stencils in a folder or large envelope with a proof of the design printed on the outside.

Stencils should be kept pressed flat at all times. You may set a few books or magazines on top of the folders, but if you are building a large collection, a heavy cardboard portfolio with side flaps is a great asset. A good one will allow you to transport your collection anywhere without worry and store it neatly.

The paper stencil

There are good reasons both for and against paper for stencils. All the designs in this book have been executed with acetate or Mylar stencils, but some could have been stenciled successfully with stencils of opaque or translucent paper.

Easier to cut than acetate, paper is relatively inexpensive and readily available, and is particularly adaptable to some special techniques (see Chapter 9). Paper also folds and bends more easily than acetate. However, stencils made of paper deteriorate rapidly, absorb paint, and cannot be adequately cleaned. A torn or broken paper stencil cannot be repaired successfully. Tracing complex designs requiring several stencils is considerably more difficult if the material is not transparent. In addition, designs that require more than one opaque or two translucent stencils can be registered only by using a system of notches instead of registration marks.

The most practical use of paper stencils is for single-stencil designs. Oaktag is relatively sturdy, but if the design is to be repeated many times across a surface, it is wise to cut several stencils at the same time to use as replacements when the first ones wear out.

Registration by the notch system

Stencils of translucent paper may be traced and registered in ink if the design requires no more than three stencils. More elaborate designs, and stencils made of oaktag or other opaque materials, must be registered with notches instead. Small notches made in the edge of each stencil permit the use of as many stencils as necessary to complete the design. If you prepare the stencils properly, you will not run into registration problems.

To make the notches, you will need carbon paper, tracing paper, sharp pencils, and masking tape, in addition to the stencil material itself.

Notching stacked stencil paper.

Tracing the design onto stencil paper.

1. Trace the complete design onto a sheet of tracing paper.
2. Decide how many stencils the design requires and select a corresponding number of pieces of stencil paper.
3. Cut the tracing paper and stencil sheets to the same size. Be sure to make them large enough to leave a 1″ margin around the design.
4. Tape the tracing paper and sheets of stencil paper securely together in a single stack and cut a V notch through them all, in the upper left-hand and lower right-hand corners.

5. Take one of the stencil paper sheets and tape the design onto it, matching the notches. Slip the carbon paper between the tracing paper and the stencil material and trace all the parts that belong on Stencil 1. Mark the stencil with its number and color.
6. Repeat this process for each consecutive stencil, lining up the notches carefully and taping down the tracing paper and the stencil securely. When you have traced the complete design onto its various stencils and cut them, you are ready to print.

Border design. To print this design in a single color, two stencils would be needed to eliminate the bridge, as explained on page 29.

Lining up notches and pencil marks.

7. Tape the first stencil to your surface. Draw both notches on your painting surface with a sharp pencil. Print the stencil.
8. Remove the stencil and place the next stencil down, lining up the notches with the pencil marks. Tape the stencil securely and print it.
9. Continue this process with all the stencils, always placing them by means of the penciled notch marks. When the design has been completed, erase the pencil marks from the surface.

This notch system should be followed whenever you are using acrylic paints. The water in the acrylic paint dissolves ink so the method of registration employed with japan paints cannot be used in conjunction with acrylics. If your stencil material is vinyl, the notch system of registration is preferred because ink does not adhere well to vinyl.

5. Stenciling Technique

Beautiful stenciling is a testimony that the artist–craftsman is in full command of his technique at all times. When you become the master of your brush, you have it in your power to determine the mood, the style, and the effect your work will have, so that the result will never be a matter of chance.

Perfect prints can be achieved by everyone, but no amount of skill or talent will insure beautiful stenciling unless the proper paints and brushes are used. Japan colors handle more easily and make possible a greater variety of shadings and nuances in tone than any other kind of paint. Acrylic paints are less versatile in effect, and their particular qualities require special techniques, which are discussed on page 91.

Below are three stencil prints. Study the difference.

Print too dry   Print too wet   Perfect print

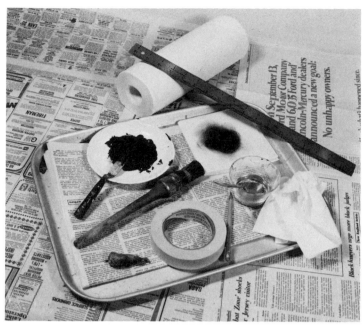

Equipment assembled on a tray.

Time

Select a time when you won't have any interruptions. Leaving your work for only five minutes may cause paints and brushes to dry out, wasting valuable time and disrupting concentration. Try to plan the work session so you can finish with at least one color or one stencil completely without rushing.

Work area

Begin each session by setting up your materials in an orderly manner. Preparation and cleaning up are both important, and their role in stenciling should not be minimized. Allow fifteen minutes to set up your materials and a minimum of fifteen minutes to clean up.

Stenciling is a clean and tidy craft. If your work space is well organized, you don't need much room. A card table covered with a plastic cloth and some clean newspaper does nicely as a workbench. Objects to be stenciled vary greatly in size. The object itself will determine the amount of additional space needed. Whether it is a small box or a chest of drawers, you will want to be in a comfortable working position. Choose a place where the light is good, where you won't feel crowded, and where you don't have to bend or strain your back unnecessarily. A wastebasket nearby for soiled tissues and paper towels is essential to help keep your work space free and clear.

Materials

Get your basic materials together, including stencils, brushes (one for each color), japan paints, a small glass bowl for turpentine, teaspoon, palette knife, roll of 1″ masking tape, paper towels, facial tissues, saucers, and brown wrapping paper, shelf paper, or any large piece of unwrinkled paper for making stencil proofs.

Mixing the paint

Once the work area has been set up, begin by mixing the paint. Stir japan paint well with a spoon before use because medium and pigment tend to separate. If the paint is in a tube, knead it well before squeezing any paint out. Put a very small amount (about half a teaspoon) of paint in a saucer. Add two or three drops of turpentine and, using a palette knife, mix thoroughly, working out the mixture until no puddle of turpentine is left anywhere in the saucer. The paint should be the consistency of soft but not melted butter. If you plan to mix a special shade with more than one color, add the colors a very small amount at a time, to prevent mixing more than you need for the job. An enormous amount of space can be stenciled with a scant amount of paint. Only a trace of paint is needed on the brush; more will seep under the stencil. The stenciled print dries to the touch immediately after application, and this same fast drying is going on in the saucer. Check the mixture every three or four minutes to be sure it isn't getting too dry. As the paint dries out in the saucer, it will lose its shiny wetness and appear dull. Two or three drops of turpentine added to the paint with a spoon and then well blended with the palette knife will leave the mixture as good as new. Checking consistency becomes automatic as you grow aware of how the paint should look and feel when you dip your brush into it.

Removing surplus paint from the brush.

Printing the stencil.

Brush technique

You have now seen what a perfect print should look like, and how it will appear if it is too wet or too dry. If you follow directions, you can turn out a perfect print every time.

Always remove surplus paint from the brush after dipping it in the paint mixture. The amount of paint on the bristles greatly affects the brushwork. A good-quality paper towel is by far the best material for this procedure. You will know when the brush is in perfect readiness by the mark it leaves on the paper towel. It should have a soft, shaded quality. Stains or blobs of color mean that there is still too much paint on your brush. Continue rubbing until you arrive at the stage where the rubbings have an even, shaded look.

Hold the brush as if it were a pencil, with fingers close to the bristles. The stenciling motion uses the entire arm, but the wrist remains flexible and relaxed. The fingers of the other hand follow along to make sure the stencil lies flat so that the bristles will not snag on parts of the stencil. It is not necessary to use a pouncing or stippling movement to fill in the stencil shapes, or to grasp the stencil brush as though it were a dagger. This is not only wearying; it destroys the command and ease needed to bring about a beautiful stencil print.

Filling in the print

A stencil print is most beautiful when it shows some degree of variation, but the total effect must have an all-over consistency. Avoid concentrating on one small area at a time. Instead, work the stencil brush in broad, circular movements both clockwise and counterclockwise until the shapes are gradually filled in. Stenciling is a process of building up the color very slowly, rather than putting it on thickly and then trying to rub it away. The stencil forms

should always have a sharp, crisp outline. Think in terms of establishing the contours of the shape first, working your way toward the center.

Every shape in a design plays a role in the total picture. Intensity provides dramatic impact, and a delicate fading out harmonizes the whole design. This is where the craftsman becomes the artist. Whether simple or complex, a stencil design is a living thing. One of the great rewards of good stenciling is the knowledge that you can give life to each and every design element. If you remember this as you stencil, you will find your work full of vitality and originality.

Wet prints

Too much paint on the stencil brush or a paint mixture that is too thin and runny causes paint to seep under the stencil. Shapes become blurred instead of clearly defined. Because the paint does not dry fast enough, smudges appear. If the print seems too wet, stop stenciling and remove the stencil to see just how bad the damage is. If it is hardly visible, chances are it will not be noticed in the over-all effect. Check your paint to be sure you haven't added too much turpentine to the japan paint mixture. Then check your brush and see if you removed enough paint before starting to stencil. It is always a good idea, when starting a print, to lift a corner of the stencil and examine what is actually happening underneath. An ounce of prevention is worth a pound of cure.

Dry prints

A dry print indicates that the paint or brush has become too dry. This may happen if you try to stencil too big an area without replenishing the paint on your brush or if you walk away from the

Subtle shading harmonizes the elements of a design and adds to the beauty and individuality of the stenciling.

work a few minutes. Dry, faded-out shapes do not have a clean, sharp outline. While not actually messy, they create confusion in the design.

Stop stenciling and dip your stencil brush in the paint mixture. Wipe the brush well and gently re-stencil any shapes that appeared too dry. If this does not solve the problem, clean the brush with a paper towel moistened with turpentine; *do not* immerse it in turpentine during the stenciling.

Correcting mistakes

All sorts of mistakes may be made while stenciling, from paint seeping under the stencil to miscalculation of the design. Whatever happens, don't panic. Most mishaps can be promptly corrected.

Save a small jar of the background paint to touch up any smudges or small errors after you are through stenciling and are appraising the whole work. If you have a stain background, apply a protective coat of flat varnish over it *before* stenciling begins so that any errors may be repaired.

Keep your hands as free of paint as possible. The fingers that hold the stencils always pick up some paint. Moisten a tissue with turpentine to clean them.

Keep a kneaded eraser handy. You can use it to correct many small mistakes if you catch them before the paint dries hard. Roll the eraser to a sharp point and gently swab off the mistake. It won't smear, because the eraser picks up the unwanted paint. Prints that are too dark can be lightened by using a kneaded eraser as a blotter. Just press it on the print once or twice before the paint becomes too dry.

Running-under

This is perhaps the most common problem in stenciling. There are several ways to correct it. The method of correction is determined by the severity of the case, but remedy the mistake immediately. If the paint is still moist enough to pick up with the kneaded eraser, you will find this method the fastest. If the paint is already dry, try shifting the stencil over just a hairbreadth and re-stencil the shape, being careful not to let it get too dark.

If the running-under is extensive, remove it with a facial tissue very slightly moistened with turpentine. Protect the rest of the print from smudging by putting small pieces of masking tape along the contour of the shapes to be guarded before wiping away the unwanted paint.

Miscalculations in the design

Misjudgments in the arrangement or placement of part of a design may not become apparent until a large portion of the stenciling has been done. Such miscalculation can be corrected easily by using any of the methods suggested for repairing running-under. Any severe cases that remain unnoticed until the whole surface has been stenciled may be remedied by washing down the entire surface with turpentine and beginning all over again. (This is not as formidable as it sounds.) Wipe the surface dry with paper towels, and if no trace of japan pigment remains, you can re-stencil immediately. If it is not entirely clean, try washing the surface down more thoroughly or repaint the surface. Happily, the latter extreme solution is seldom necessary.

If the miscalculation was only partial, block off the salvageable areas around the unsatisfactory portion with tape and wash down only that section.

Design revision

Deficiencies in design that are revealed during stenciling often can be revised by improvisation. Using parts of your stencil, fill in vacant spaces and unbalanced areas with small elements of the design. The final effect is often more charming than if no error had occurred; it adds a very spontaneous personal touch.

Caked stencil brush

If you are doing an extensive amount of stenciling in one session, the brush may become gummed up and stiff. To clean it, remove the caked paint quickly and easily by pouring a teaspoonful of turpentine onto a piece of folded paper towel and wipe the sides of the brush all around until the bristles appear clean. This way the brush regains its flexibility, and you will be able quickly to resume a smooth, easygoing pace. If the bristles still seem a bit too moist, give them a good squeeze with a facial tissue. Do not immerse the brush in turpentine or thinner to remove caking while you are working; if you do, you won't be able to use it again right away. Turpentine takes a long time to evaporate from the upper bristles, and it has an annoying way of slowly working down to the tips of the bristles, causing running-under problems.

Clogged stencils

If the paint mixture is kept at the right consistency, clogging is not likely to occur except on very large projects in which the stencils are being used continuously for several hours. When the stencil brush is kept in good working condition, neither caked nor gummy, the friction of the bristles on the stencil assists in checking paint accumulation. When too much paint collects on the stencil, the cutout

Cleaning up runs. Tape keeps the print from smudging.

shapes become smaller and you begin to lose the transparency of the stencil. Lay your brush aside a few moments and give your stencils a good cleaning.

Misplaced stencils

Stencils often get misplaced, especially acetate ones. If you have just finished using a stencil, leave the tape on it and stick it on the wall or at the edge of the card table where you can spot it right away, ready for use until it is time to clean it and put it away.

Muscle fatigue

You are bound to feel a bit stiff when you are using a new set of muscles for the first time. If you are in a normal standing or sitting position while stenciling, you will be all right, but a lot of bending, stretching, or crouching will make you wonder what happened when the next morning comes around. Soak in a hot bath just as soon after the stenciling as possible. Don't wait until bedtime when stiffness has already set in. When you're stenciling a floor, try to limit work to no more than two or three hours the first day. Five hours in any one day should be the maximum.

Saving time and energy

Completing all of the decorating to be done with one stencil before going on to the next one is always faster than alternating two stencils back and forth, especially when each stencil represents a different color. On a very large project, such as an all-over design on a floor, this may become monotonously tiring, and you may want to break the work down into large sections to be completed one at a time, just for variety's sake, and without much loss in efficiency.

Cleaning up

Always clean up your materials when you are through working for the day. If you leave them until the next day or only a few hours later, you will be faced with a task twice as difficult. Japan paint will clean off rapidly and easily before it sets; after that it takes real elbow grease to get rid of it. On stencils, a gentle wipe has a great advantage over a strenuous scrubbing. Cleaning your materials promptly and carefully and leaving the work area tidy and well-organized for the next session will give you an encouraging feeling of having done your best, with no worries to spoil your sense of accomplishment.

Cleaning stencil brushes

Empty coffee cans are very suitable for cleaning brushes, but any wide-mouth jar will serve nicely. Mineral spirits, which cost about half as much as turpentine, are needed in generous amounts for the rinses. Take three clean coffee cans and mark them "One," "Two," and "Three" for the three rinses. You may use the thinner for several cleanings, but always keep to the same sequence of first, second, and third rinse. Pour enough thinner into each can so that all the bristles will be immersed. Swish the brushes well in the first rinse and squeeze out as much thinner as possible on the inside of the can or on a paper towel. Repeat several times. Drop the

41

Cleaning brushes.

Cleaning a stencil.

brushes into the second can and repeat the process, and again in the third. Dry the brushes fairly well on a paper towel and take them to the kitchen sink for a bath. Another coffee can will suffice for this. Use warm water with soap or a mild liquid detergent. Harsh detergents ruin the bristles. Rinse in several waters until you know the brushes are clean, then dry them with a clean rag or paper towel. Stand them up to dry thoroughly overnight before using them again. If the bristles have a tendency to spread out, put a rubber band around them while they are still damp. Stencil brushes have a long life, but when the bristles wear down from use so that they lose their flexibility, throw them away.

Cleaning the stencils

Remove all masking tape from the stencils. Pour about a quarter of a cup of turpentine or mineral spirits into a clean bowl. Spread newspapers on your worktable and cover them with several layers of paper towels. Place the stencil on the towels and, using a tissue moistened with turpentine, wipe with a firm but gentle motion. Pay strict attention to the outlines of each shape, never wiping against the edge because you might bend or break off part of the stencil. Always keep the stencil flat on the paper towels, controlling it with one hand. Don't hurry—

you will spend twice the time repairing the stencil if it breaks. Change the tissue as often as needed to end up with a very clean and dry stencil. Clean both sides of the stencil thoroughly. (Acetate is easily cleaned, but paper stencils absorb much paint which can never be entirely removed.) When the paper towels under the stencil become soiled, replace them with clean ones. Return the stencils to their folder for safekeeping.

Cleaning paint saucers

One way to be thrifty in stenciling is to put aside for reuse all facial tissues and paper towels that don't have heavy gobs of paint on them. These can serve for cleaning saucers. Pour some mineral spirits into the paint-clogged saucer and use your collection of semisoiled tissues and towels to wipe the saucer clean. You might need a little extra help from the palette knife. To remove paint that has already dried hard, use a teaspoonful of liquid paint remover. It will soften the paint in minutes, but wear rubber gloves to protect your hands.

If you have a large amount of paint left over on the saucer and you plan to use it in the next day or two, float about a teaspoonful of turpentine over the paint mixture. Do not stir it. Cover the saucer tightly with plastic wrap and put it aside until you are ready to resume painting.

6. Measuring and Placing Designs

There are several methods of accurately arranging designs on a surface, from a simple placement by eye to the very precise measuring and marking required by continuous all-over designs. Measurements for decorating a surface should be planned in advance, not devised as you go along. Unless the design is to be placed by eye, some kind of marks are needed to indicate where the design should be placed.

Placing by eye

Designs placed casually often lend a naïve charm to informal objects. If the situation calls for such simplicity, single designs and borders may be printed without measuring or marking off the surface beforehand.

Placing by proofs

A little extra visual help may be all that is needed to place a design attractively. Stencil a number of paper proofs and move them about on the surface to be decorated until you achieve an arrangement to your liking. When you are ready to proceed with the stenciling, simply replace the paper proof with the stencil. (See Project 2, page 112.)

Guidelines

To place designs on a surface according to a predetermined plan, guidelines may be needed. If it is simply a matter of keeping a border running straight, these lines may be needed only on the surface to be stenciled. However, to center a single design or to place accurately an all-over repeat design, guidelines should be marked on the stencil in ink, with corresponding ones lightly drawn on the surface in pencil or chalk so that they can be easily erased. Measure and mark the two sets of guidelines so that they coincide when the stencil is set on the surface for printing.

Centering a design

To center a design, make short vertical and horizontal guidelines across the middle of the surface, forming an upright cross or plus mark there. Make the same mark on the stencil at the center of the design, and place it directly over the one on the surface as you print.

Using pencil marks to place a design.

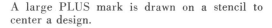

A large PLUS mark is drawn on a stencil to center a design.

The plus mark accurately places the print on intersecting guidelines.

Spacing a border design.

Arranging border designs

Before starting to stencil a border, figure how many times the repeat will fit into the chosen area. Measure the width of a single repeat of the design. Measure the length of the border or surface. Divide the width of the design into the entire length of the border. If there is to be a space between each repeat, be sure to include this in your measuring. Mark a pencil or chalk guideline lengthwise on the surface and draw corresponding guidelines on the stencil. After you have calculated the number of repeats, make marks along the surface guideline to show where each repeat should be placed.

Arranging border designs always raises the question of whether the final repeat of the design will be complete or incomplete when you reach the end of the border area. If necessary to make the design come out evenly on both ends, you may simply expand or reduce spaces between each repeat to make an even distribution possible. A continuous design may be completed gracefully by blocking out some parts of the design in the final repeat, or by filling in the final space with an attractive rearrangement of some of the shapes in the stencil, instead of using the full repeat.

Placement marks

Any continuous design (such as a vine) that has no space between repeats requires placement marks

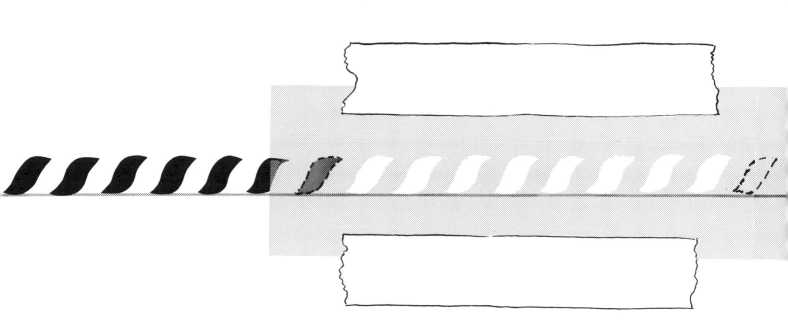

To link repeats of a continuous design, make placement marks at either end of the stencil as shown above.

to link the design shapes of each print to those of the preceding print. These marks may be made at both ends of the stencil so that it can be moved in either direction for printing. If the design uses more than one stencil, you need to make the placement marks on Stencil 1 only. To make the marks, make the first print from Stencil 1. Move the stencil into position to start the next print. Trace some of the already printed shapes onto the edge of Stencil 1 at the point where it overlaps the first print. Do the same at the opposite end of the print. Subsequent stencils (if the design includes them) are placed over the prints made by Stencil 1 by means of their register marks. To keep the design running straight, guidelines may be needed as well.

Placing all-over designs

If you examine patterned wallpaper or lengths of fabric, you will see that the design is repeated again and again in a definite order. In stenciling, the dimensions of such a pattern must be calculated in advance so that, when it is printed, each repeat is placed properly in relation to the identical one alongside it. This requires guidelines on the stencil to correspond with squares (or rectangles) marked off on the surface, each to contain one design repeat.

In preparing stencils for an all-over design, it is important that the design be accurately placed on the stencil to fall within the units of the grid. Using

graph paper or a drawing board and T square, mark on the stencil the same square or rectangle that is to be marked on the surface. When the stencils are cut, print trial proofs to make sure that the design properly meets all four adjoining prints. Correct any mismatches. Placement marks made on all four sides of the stencil may be used in addition to the square drawn on the stencil. This helps verify correct placement of the stencil when it is printed repeatedly.

Squaring off a surface

To square off the surface, establish the center first, then work out from the center to the four sides, marking the squares as you go. This will distribute the design so that opposite sides will match.

If the surface you are squaring off is not too large, use a ruler or yardstick to draw the lines, and a T square or triangle to help keep the intersections square. Large areas, such as a floor or wall, should be squared off with a plumb line or chalk box.

Placing paper stencils in a squared-off pattern

Paper or oaktag stencils may be used with a squared-off repeat pattern. Draw the squares or rectangles on the stencil as well as on the surface, bringing them all the way out to the edge. You will then be able to match these guidelines up with those drawn on the surface.

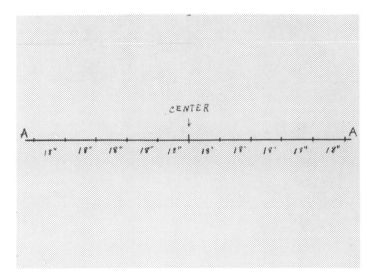

Squaring off a floor. Make a straight line (AA) across the center.

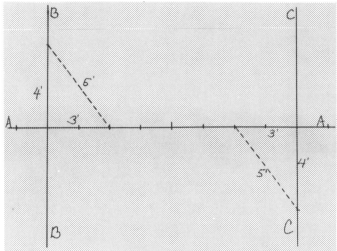

Draw parallel lines BB and CC at right angles to AA.

Squaring off a floor

Any floor that requires a regular all-over repeat of a design must be squared off with a plumb line before stenciling can begin. The process of squaring off is based on a few simple rules:

1. A straight line can be drawn accurately using only two points. More are unnecessary.
2. All right angles must be made perfectly because a slight error at the beginning magnifies to a large one when the lines are extended to the end of the floor.
3. Start from the center of the room in marking and work out to the edges; this minimizes any errors.
4. Accuracy is important. Keep your pencils sharp, use a metal ruler if possible, and always correct any slight error at once.

If you observe these principles, you can invent your own general procedure. For example, say you want to make a grid of 18″ squares. First, mark the centers of any two opposite walls, and using the plumb line, snap your line through these two points. Call this line AA. It will remain unchanged as a base for all the following steps. (If the design will look better lined up with the cracks between the floor boards, put the first line along or parallel to a crack in the middle of the room.)

Next, find and mark the center of AA, and measuring in both directions from this center, mark 18″ sections along the line.

Construct two lines at perfect right angles to AA through two of these 18″ points. Choose an 18″ mark at either end of AA and snap lines through each of them parallel to the ends of the room. Call these lines BB and CC. These may not be entirely square. Check the accuracy of BB and CC, using the 3-4-5 formula described on page 47. Correct them until they lie in a perfect right angle to line AA. The lines are laid down in relation to each other; do not use the walls as your guide. Walls are too often out of line, even in new houses.

Do not be discouraged by the slow process of erasing and resnapping lines. It is worthwhile being careful. Once the lines are accurately placed, the rest of the job is fast and easy. (In some informal settings the 3-4-5 formula need not be rigidly followed. The charm of many Early American floors does not depend on perfect accuracy in design placement.)

After you have drawn BB and CC, measure off 18″ intervals along them, starting from AA and working out. This will provide the points needed to snap lines parallel to AA all across the floor.

Select one of these last lines as far as possible from AA (call it DD). Measure off 18″ sections along it. Now you are ready to complete the whole floor by snapping lines through points on AA and DD. When these lines (EE) are finished, the floor is squared off and ready to be stenciled.

Following this same procedure, the grid could

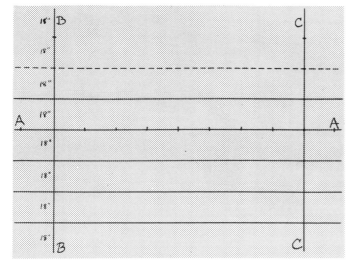

Mark off BB and CC in equal segments and draw
lines parallel to AA.

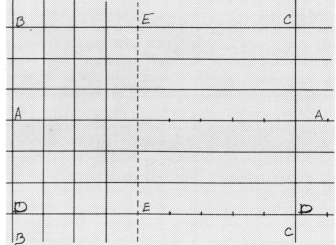

Mark off DD in equal segments and draw lines
parallel to BB and CC.

be marked off in rectangles instead of squares, in
any desired size.

Using a plumb line or chalk box

A plumb line is very helpful when you need precise, straight measurements on large areas such as
walls and floors. Two people are needed to snap
a plumb line. The device is held firmly by one person while the other pulls the chalk-coated string
out. The string is pulled very taut and snapped or
plucked in the middle, leaving a perfect, straight
chalk line where it is needed. The string may then
be rewound (and shaken if necessary) to coat the
string evenly for snapping the next line. Practice
a few snaps before you begin the job, because an
overzealous snap dispenses more chalk than you
need.

To mark white or very pale surfaces, mix blue
chalk with the white in the box. The chalk lines
should be dark enough to be easily visible, but not
so dark that they are difficult to remove. When the
stenciling is finished, and before it is varnished,
remove the chalk marks with a clean rag or a
kneaded eraser.

Confirming right angles (the 3-4-5 formula)

The 3-4-5 formula is based on the familiar Pytha-
gorean theorem: In a right triangle the square of
the hypotenuse equals the sum of the squares of
the other two sides. For our purposes, this means
that if there are two lines at perfect right angles to
each other, and you measure 3′ along one and 4′
along the other from their crossing point, then a
line drawn or measured between the 3′ and the 4′
marks should be exactly 5′ long. If this line does
not measure *exactly* 5′, you *do not* have a perfect
right angle. A measurement of more than 5′ indicates too wide an angle, and less than 5′ a too narrow one. You can double or triple all the measurements for even better results, provided the room is
big enough to hold them; for example: 6-8-10 or
9-12-15. The greater the measurement, the more
accurate the test.

A draftsmen's or a carpenters' square is not as
reliable as the 3-4-5 formula because the square is
not big enough to check the accuracy of the arms of
the angle as they diverge from the meeting point out
toward the ends of the room. By the time a hairbreadth of error at the center is carried out to the
end of the room, it may be magnified to an inch
or two.

Marking walls

In houses where the walls are uneven, you may
need to establish some truly vertical lines as a
guide to accurate measurement of the surface. Sus-
pend the plumb line from the upper part of the
wall so it dangles free of the floor or baseboard.
A pushpin makes an inconspicuous hole and can be
used in place of a nail to hang the plumb line.

Make only enough vertical plumb lines to insure the accuracy of the other measurements. The
horizontal lines and the remaining vertical lines
can be made with a ruler and a triangle, measuring
from the plumb lines and marking the lines lightly
with a pencil.

A continuous border design.

Marking borders

A floor may be decorated with borders or with a combination of borders and an all-over pattern. In the latter case the border should be marked off first, using a plumb line to make the lines.

When you are combining a border with an all-over pattern and want the all-over pattern to conclude in the same way at either end, mark the surface in a grid of squares which correspond in size to one repeat of the design. Begin marking from the middle of the floor and work outward to the border. Should the all-over design be incomplete where it meets the border, do not be disturbed. Tape a strip of paper or cardboard over the border and print up to it. (See page 125.)

Stenciling stripes

Stripes of any size may be made quickly and reliably by using acetate or stencil board strips to make a clean edge. (Mylar or stencil paper is not heavy enough.) The use of masking tape as a guide should be avoided, if possible, as the paint tends to run under and make a ragged edge. If the stripe is short, it may be cut out like any other stencil shape and printed end-to-end. For stripes on a larger scale, use two strips of heavy stencil material, cutting them the full length of the stencil sheet.

1. Draw the outline of the stripe on the stenciling surface. If the surface is a large one, such as a floor, use a plumb line to make the outline of the stripe.
2. Cut two strips of stencil material the entire length of the sheet. Include one of the outside edges of the sheet on each piece, because these machine-cut edges are straighter than handmade ones.
3. Put masking tape along the hand-cut sides and at the ends of the strips, leaving the straight edges of the strip free.
4. Tape these strips down parallel to each other, matching their machine-cut edges with the lines drawn on the surface.
5. Stencil in the space between the strips with a stencil brush or a roller.
6. Stop just before you reach the end of the section of stripe and move the whole arrangement to the next position so that it slightly overlaps the previously printed one. The paint should not overlap, so shade it out to nothingness at the end of each section.

Stenciled stripes may be left plain, or they may be stenciled over with a design, as in Project 5.

Print all-over designs working outward from the center across a grid premeasured to allow even distribution of the design.

48

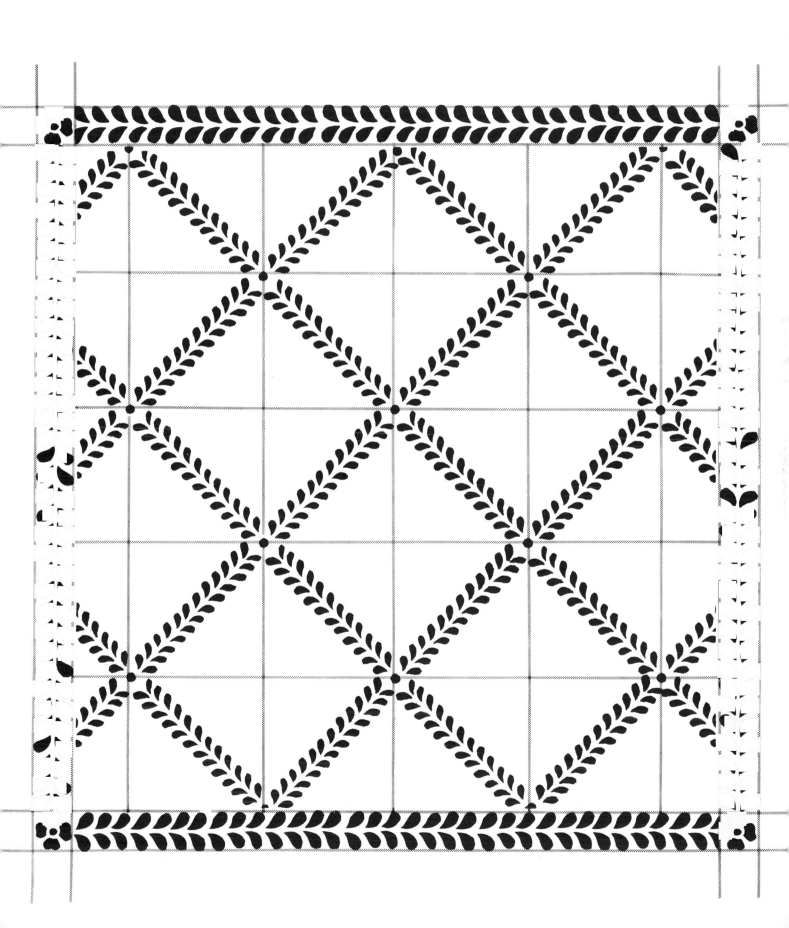

Handling corners

Border designs that lead into corners can be handled in several ways:

1. *Butt the border at the corner,* placing it at right angles to the adjoining border.

2. *Design a special corner piece,* choosing motifs derived from the border. Always stencil the corners first, then measure and space the border stencils to meet them.

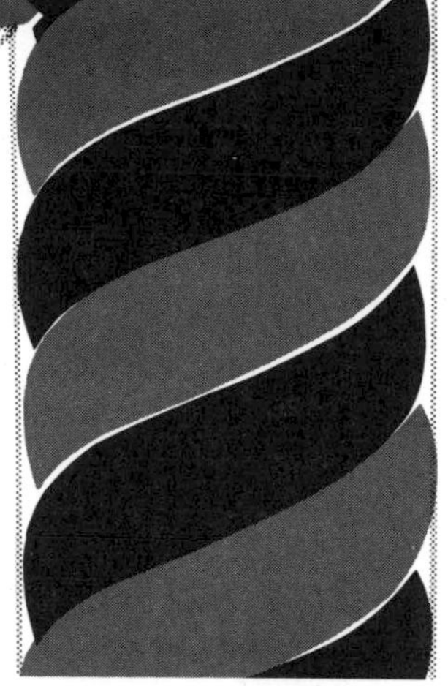

3. *Miter the corner of the design.* Draw a
   diagonal line from the inner to the outer
   corner of the border and place masking
   tape snugly along one side of this line.
   Stencil up to the tape, then remove the
   tape and place it on the other side of the
   diagonal line. Now stencil up to the tape
   from the opposite direction.

4. *"Piece" the corner.* Block out shapes in
   some parts of the design and fill in
   shapes in other parts, wherever a gap
   occurs, to carry the design around the
   corner without interruption. This solution works particularly well with vine
   borders.

To practice piecing, trace one complete unit of
the design on page 48 and fit it around the corner,
as shown here. You will quickly see how pieces can
be blocked out and filled in to make a graceful
corner.

Piecing the vine border to turn a corner.

Flexible stencil bent to go into a corner.

Acetate stencil hinged to fit an awkward area.

Using a smaller stencil to print near a molding.

Stenciling in awkward areas

Sometimes stencils cannot be placed flat on the decorating surface because a molding, baseboard, or other obstacle is in the way. If the stencil is not perfectly flat, the print will be incomplete or fuzzy. If this is so pronounced that it is objectionable, there are various solutions:

1. *Bend the stencil.* Mylar or paper stencils can be simply bent or folded right at the edge of the design so that the adjacent margin may be placed flush against the obstacle, while the design lies flat on the printing surface.

2. *Hinge the stencil.* Acetate cannot be bent by hand. Instead you must place a steel ruler on the margin of the stencil about $1/8''$ from the edge of the design. Using the ruler as a guide, cut along it with a utility knife. Do not remove this margin strip. Place two long pieces of transparent tape lengthwise over the cut on both sides of the stencil. The stencil is still intact but can now easily be bent against the obstacle.

3. *Cut small stencils.* Those parts of the design that cannot be placed flat may be duplicated on small pieces of stencil material. Fit these smaller stencils close to the wall or molding and cover any parts of the surface that might be smudged with masking tape.

4. *Complete the design by hand.* If the area is so small or difficult to reach that smaller stencils will not solve the problem, paint in the shapes by hand with a fine-point sable brush and stencil paint slightly thinned with turpentine.

Blocking out design areas

There are three ways to block out parts of the design on the stencil:

1. Cover with masking tape or cardboard the section of surface on which you do not wish the stencil print to appear. Remove the masking tape or cardboard after printing.
2. Mask the unwanted shapes with a piece of paper or cardboard taped to the stencil. Remove the tape carefully to avoid tearing the stencil.
3. Place a small piece of cardboard over the shapes you want to omit and hold it there with one hand while stenciling. This untaped mask can be swiftly moved from place to place to make occasional variations in the design.

Filling in

To fill in areas at the sides or ends of a continuous border or all-over pattern, print small elements of the design from the existing stencil. Block out unwanted shapes with tape or cardboard, arrange the stencil on the surface so that the desired shapes fit attractively against those already printed, and print.

If the stencil is large and unwieldy, or the space awkward to reach, make small stencils of the individual shapes needed to fill out the scheme and move them around as needed to complete the arrangement satisfactorily.

The procedures involved in measuring and marking walls, floors, or other surfaces for decorating are not difficult; they are only time-consuming, and the time is always well spent.

7. Backgrounds and Finishes

Walls, Furniture, Floors, and Tinware

The nature of the surface to be decorated is an important part of the total scheme of any stenciling project. The design you select and the effect you want to produce with it help to determine the way this surface should be prepared for stenciling and finished afterward.

Some stenciling is done directly on materials that are not prepared beforehand. In most cases these materials need no finish. This is true of lamp shades, woven mats and baskets, leather, fabric, window shades, and natural fibers, including burlap. However, the handling of walls, furniture, floors, and tinware can differ widely.

Preparing walls
Most wall surfaces should be painted before they are stenciled. This includes plaster, sheetrock (plasterboard), and paneled walls. In very old houses the original plaster walls are often in a deplorable condition, held together with several layers of wallpaper which, if removed, would expose nothing but crumbling plaster. If you suspect this would happen, leave the paper; cover it with flat oil-base paint. Spackle the seams first so they won't leave any telltale marks. If you do this properly, no one will be any the wiser.

When you are ready to paint the walls, consider texture as well as color. If you apply the paint with a roller, it will produce a pebbly look. You might prefer using a brush to produce a smoother background. Specially prepared texture paints can be a great help in covering imperfections. We recommend flat paint as a background for wall decoration. Avoid chalk-white by having the paint tinted slightly with raw umber.

Finishing walls
Painted and stenciled walls do not need a finish unless one is desired for a special effect. In Project 3, a design inspired by antique tiles, the stenciling was covered with two coats of high-gloss varnish making the stenciled tiles look astonishingly real. The smooth finish protects them from muddy-pawed dogs and grubby-fingered children. When you want extra protection but do not want a gloss effect, use a flat varnish over the stenciling. Bear in mind the fact that all varnish has a slightly amber cast.

Stenciled walls can be washed after being allowed to set for a period of at least six months. Use a mild soap-and-water solution (not detergent) to clean off soiled spots. Wipe gently with a sponge.

Wood paneling
Wood paneling should be treated in the same way as furniture. When you choose your designs for a paneled wall, take into consideration the vertical or horizontal direction of the planks or panels.

Preparation of furniture
Wood furniture offers the widest range of possible surface treatment. If the design is contemporary in feeling or has delicate, fine shapes, the surface usually should be smooth. If you want the piece to look rustic or primitive or very old, then a rough-textured surface would be more appropriate.

Backgrounds for stenciling may be stained, glazed, or painted. Whichever you use, one basic rule applies to them all: *the surface you stencil on cannot be slick.* It is permissible to use a satin or semigloss varnish or paint, but never, never gloss. If you have to use anything glossy, sand it down slightly to take off the gloss. If all traces of wax have not been thoroughly removed, wash the piece down well with denatured alcohol and steel wool, or use a commercial wax solvent, following instructions carefully.

Staining backgrounds

Only raw wood should be stained. The stain allows wood grain and knotholes to show through the color. Be sure to take this into consideration when you choose your design. Have the wood sanded before staining and re-sand if the stain raises the grain.

The best stains to work with are ones that don't streak when they are applied. These are generally the oil-base stains, and a great variety of them are sold in paint and hardware stores everywhere. Many oil-base stains penetrate, seal, and protect the wood. This is all to the good. If you don't like any of the ready-mixed shades, you may purchase a natural stain and tint it yourself with japan paints or a Universal Colorant. When a great deal of pigment is added to stain or sealer, it takes on the characteristics of a translucent paint coat and can be used as a glaze. Be sure the stain is well mixed and test the color where it won't show before beginning to apply the stain over the whole area. Stain may be applied with either a rag or a brush.

On a stained surface stencil paint may be absorbed into the grain of the wood. This becomes a problem if you make mistakes in the stenciling and want to remove them. You can eliminate this hazard by giving the stained surface a coat of flat varnish before you start to stencil.

Painting backgrounds

Whether you are painting over raw wood or a previously painted or varnished surface, the same rules apply: sand the surface smooth and use a flat or satin-finish paint.

Two coats of paint are usually enough, but occasionally a third may be necessary. Oil- or water-base paints may both be used as a background for stenciling. Save some of the background paint for touch-ups. If you paint with a water-base paint, do not stencil with acetate stencils until the following day. Even when the paint feels dry, it may still exude damp vapors that tend to curl up acetate.

Covering bleeding knotholes

When wood (particularly pine) has not been properly kiln-dried, rings of pitch around the knotholes may bleed through the paint, especially if it is a water-base latex or acrylic paint. If the raw wood does not seem well-seasoned, seal it off with either a shellac-base primer or a coat of shellac. The shellac-base primer dries to an absolutely flat, opaque white. A light sanding to smooth the surface may be necessary after the application is dry.

Bleeding varnish

If you use a water-base paint to paint over old furniture, the varnish may bleed through. Aniline dyes were once used to darken varnish (particularly mahogany), and these old varnish stains will surely bleed through unless you either paint the piece first with a shellac-base primer or with an oil-base paint.

Gesso

Thick and pastelike, acrylic gesso can be used as a background in many ways. It may serve as a substitute for white paint or as a base coat for another paint or glaze. It can be manipulated to create textured surfaces for antiquing or as a primer coat to cover and fill in rough, pitted, or uneven wood surfaces.

Acrylic gesso may be thinned with water, or used as it comes from the can to form a solid base on cracked or porous surfaces. Once dry, it is flat, hard, and smooth.

Applying gesso

There are several ways to apply gesso, depending on the role it is to fulfill, but certain rules always apply.

1. Be sure to dip the brush in water to moisten—but not saturate—the bristles before dipping it in gesso. A two- or three-inch nylon brush is suitable. Dip only about one-third the length of the bristles into the gesso.
2. Never apply gesso on the shadowed side of a piece of furniture. Keep the top and side of the working surface to the light so that you can see the brushstrokes.
3. After painting gesso on each side, look at all the adjacent sides in slanting light, to be sure beads of paint have not piled up over the edges. If so, flatten them with the brush while they are still wet.

Applying gesso to well-lighted surface.

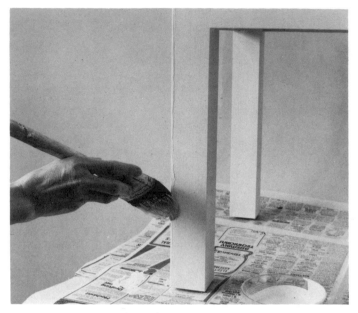

Flattening built-up ridges of gesso.

4. Wipe the brush with a damp paper towel from time to time to keep the bristles from caking.

5. When you stop work for an extended period or overnight, wash the brush with soap and water. Clean the lid of the gesso container and close it very tightly.

Gesso as a base coat or as white paint

The heavy consistency of gesso retains brushstrokes. Keep the strokes consistently lengthwise to the side of the object you are working on; do not use a circular motion or paint at right angles to the grain of the wood or the direction of the surface. This is especially important if you do not plan to sand each coat to satin smoothness. Watch for little brush marks at the ends of the strokes and smooth them out as they occur.

Keep the gesso as thick as possible for smooth coating. If the coat of gesso is too thin, it will be removed by the sanding. Two coats of gesso are usually sufficient to cover raw wood, making it a nice opaque white.

Sanding gesso

After each coat of gesso has dried thoroughly, sand it down. Gentle sanding modifies the brushstrokes; a more thorough sanding brings it down to a satin smoothness. In either case, spread sheets of newspaper under the piece to be sanded and begin with a medium (#80 Production) sandpaper and finish up with fine (#120 Production). Replace each piece of sandpaper as soon as it becomes clogged with gesso powder. If traces of gesso beads

remain, sand them off. Sand excess gesso off all corners and edges to prevent any later chipping at these very vulnerable points. Vacuum up all gesso dust from the sanding. Wipe with a tack cloth to pick up any remaining dust.

Gesso as a base for antiquing and distressing

Its thick consistency makes gesso ideal for creating interesting background textures. Be sure your work is well lighted and keep a sharp eye on the brushstrokes. Any antiquing applied over the gesso will emphasize the brushstroked texture and bring out any distressed effects.

Apply a coat of gesso. Allow it to dry. Apply a second undiluted coat to one side of the piece at a time. The gesso will become tacky fairly quickly. Experiment by dragging, pouncing, and scrubbing the brush in the gesso until you get a pleasing surface texture. Don't do the other sides until you are satisfied with the first one.

To exaggerate the texture, add worm holes, scratches, nicks, or gouges when the gesso begins to look dry but actually is still damp. The gesso will take such distressing readily if it is done before it becomes bone-dry. Distressing can be done with a steel file, razor blade, nails, hammer, metal chains, stones, or other hard or sharp objects. The aim is to make the piece look naturally old and worn—usually along the more prominent edges, curves, or moldings. Apply distressing to portions that would normally be subject to hard wear and accidental knocks and bruises. Antiquing will emphasize the distressing, so employ a fairly light hand unless you are after very exaggerated effects.

56

Antiquing backgrounds with turpentine and japan paint

Applied correctly to a gessoed or painted surface, this process simulates age and dirt. The surface must have a texture provided by brushstrokes or distressing to catch the antiquing mixture. This kind of antiquing is always done *before* the stenciling.

If the background color is to be antique white or ivory, the antiquing mixture is applied directly to the dry, hard gesso base. If the background is to be anything other than white, paint over the gesso with flat paint or tint the gesso itself with acrylic paint. Wait until it is thoroughly dry before beginning the antiquing process.

The amount of paint added to turpentine for antiquing is very small. To one-half pint of turpentine, add no more than one teaspoon of japan paint. The color should suggest the presence of dust and antiquity, so make tests to get the effect you want. Raw umber is safe, but any of a number of colors can be used in combination to simulate aging: black, raw umber, raw sienna, burnt sienna, burnt umber, and yellow ochre. The mixture will be thin and runny, so, if possible, turn your surface to lie flat while you are working on it so the mixture will not run down. Stir the mixture frequently, use a large paintbrush, and work swiftly. Take a clean, dry rag and lightly remove most of the liquid from the surface. The brushstrokes and distressing in the gesso will catch the mixture. Run the rag back over the surface, rapidly redepositing additional antiquing wherever you want it. Continue until the surface looks sufficiently aged, especially around corners and edges.

You will soon get the knack of putting on and taking off just enough. If the results are not satisfactory, remove the antiquing entirely with a clean rag and turpentine and start over. Allow the antiquing mixture to dry thoroughly before stenciling.

Antiquing finishes with rottenstone and wax

Rubbing with a mixture of wax and rottenstone easily adds years to your piece. Use two parts Butcher's Wax to one part rottenstone. Add turpentine for easier application. Alter the proportions of the wax and rottenstone, depending on how light or dark you want the antiquing. This process is always used *after* the stenciling, and after a coat of flat varnish has been applied to isolate the stenciling from the wax. Be sure the stenciling is completely dry before you begin to varnish, and follow the usual precautions for varnishing over stenciling given on page 59.

Smoothing out brushmarks at ends of strokes.

Sanding edges.

Creating the texture.

Removing excess antiquing mixture.

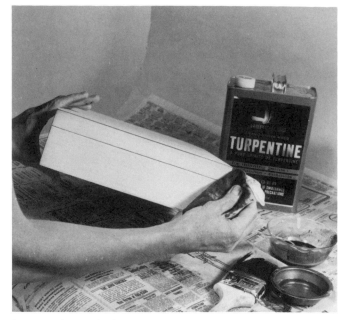

Accentuating antiquing on corners.

Choose a well-lighted area and spread news-papers under the work. For an average-dark mix-ture, put two parts Butcher's Wax and one part rottenstone in a small bowl and mix very well with a spoon. Add a few drops of turpentine to reach a consistency that can be applied with a brush. Keep this brush *only* for waxing. Brush rapidly but thor-oughly, in a lengthwise motion. The application will seem quite dark while wet.

Allow the mixture to dry completely, anywhere from one to three hours. When it is dry, it will have a smoky, hazy, somewhat dusty look. Rub the sur-face back and forth with fine steel wool (#000). The wax takes on a soft luster, while the rottenstone clings to the uneven texture provided by the brush-strokes and distressing applied earlier. The surface quickly acquires the darkened and dusty look that usually accumulates with the passage of time. Once dry, antique finish is almost impossible to remove except with turpentine and steel wool. To touch up parts that should look particularly dirty, go over them again with the mixture, but let them dry com-pletely before buffing. Treat the piece antiqued this way roughly if you wish. The more you use it the better it will look. Buff it firmly with steel wool, and use a tack cloth to dust the piece off.

Glazing

The application of a color directly over another color or white so that it appears to float above the background color is called glazing. The glaze is brushed on with strokes that allow the undercoat to show through. Glazing adds a luminous, glow-ing quality, an illusion of deeper dimension, and greater elegance. Glazing usually *precedes* stencil-ing. Doing it well takes a bit of practice. Experi-ment on a sample board, not on the object to be decorated. A basic formula for color glaze is:

  2 parts varnish (flat or semigloss)
  2 parts turpentine
  ½ part japan paint (increase the paint for a
     more intense color)

A dark glaze may be applied over a light un-dercoat, or a light glaze over a dark undercoat. Brush the mixture on the surface as you would a coat of varnish. Use even strokes but work rapidly because you want the surface to dry uniformly. *Be-fore* it dries thoroughly, and while it is still tacky, take the same brush and, applying considerable pressure, drag the brush through the glaze. Wipe the excess glaze picked up by the brush on some paper towels so that the brush will continue to streak through the glaze without reapplying it. If you should want to glaze *over* stenciling, first give the stenciled surface a coat of flat varnish to isolate it from the glaze.

Aging the design

A simple and fast method to get the stenciling to look old and worn is to rub it with steel wool or sandpaper. Apply the stencil paint very sparsely on anything you want to look really ancient. The final wearing-down is done after the entire piece has been stenciled but before it is varnished. Parts that would have been handled a great deal, such as the lid of an old chest, would be more worn than others.

Rubbing very gently with a fine-quality steel wool (#0000) or the finest sandpaper (#120 Production) will wear down the paint in a natural-looking way. Be sure the stencil paint is absolutely dry, and don't overdo the rubbing. If the background is white, use sandpaper only.

Finishing furniture with varnish

Applying a finish after you have stenciled protects the surface, adds beauty by bringing out the colors, and gives the piece a polished look. Varnish is preferred because it is easy to apply and has such excellent protective qualities. It is usually available in at least three finishes: flat, satin, and gloss.

A *flat* finish will protect the surface but leave it without any shine.
A *satin* finish simulates the soft glow of hand-rubbed wax.
A *gloss* finish provides a hard, brilliantly glasslike surface and brings out the colors more than the softer finishes.

Before varnishing, make sure the stenciling is thoroughly dry and test a small, inconspicuous section for bleeding. Stencil paint may take as long as three days or a week to dry sufficiently for varnishing. Take note that red has a tendency to bleed more than other colors and that artists' oil paint added to japan paint slows down the drying process. Stencil paint will also take longer to dry on nonporous surfaces, or if it has been very heavily applied.

If you have given the stenciling sufficient time to dry and it still shows signs of bleeding, add a light coat of shellac before varnishing. Remove all particles of dust with a tack cloth first, and apply the shellac with either a spray or brush. Shellac will not dissolve the stenciling; it will protect it from any possible disturbance by the varnish brush. Sprays should always be used very sparingly, because heavy applications will weep and run down the surface.

When you are satisfied that the stenciling is thoroughly dry and properly safe against bleeding, you are ready to varnish, following these procedures:

1. Pick up all dust with a tack cloth and work where there will be a minimum of dust in the air. Avoid varnishing under humid conditions.

2. Use a good, undiluted furniture varnish. It need not be polyurethane, but the label should specify that the varnish is impervious to water and alcohol.

3. Apply the varnish with a clean, soft brush. Work rapidly and lightly, without overbrushing, which might agitate the stencil paint, especially if you have not added an intermediate coat of shellac. When finished, wash the brush with several rinses of turpentine or mineral spirits, followed by soap and water. Reserve this brush for varnishing only.

4. For a smoother finish, rub each coat of varnish with steel wool after it has thoroughly dried. Always use a very fine (#000) steel wool. When using a high-gloss varnish, omit this rubbing on the final coat. Between coats, remove all dust particles with a tack cloth.

Varnish is also used as a medium for a glaze; to isolate backgrounds before stenciling; and to isolate stenciling from further antiquing. All varnishes have a slight amber cast. Always take this into consideration when choosing background and stencil colors.

Varnishing: rescuing disappearing designs

Nothing could be more disturbing than seeing carefully applied designs dissolving under the varnish brush. If you did not precede the varnishing with a coat of shellac, but have given the stenciling what should have been ample time to dry, and the stencil paint starts to run, stop varnishing at once.

With a cotton-tipped swab moistened with turpentine, gently remove the runs. Wait an hour or two, then lightly spray on a coat of varnish or shellac. Two light coats are better than one. If possible, set the side to be sprayed so that it is horizontal. This light sprayed-on coat protects the stencil paint from any agitation by the brush. Wait until the following day before brushing on the consecutive coats of varnish of the final finish.

Lacquer as a finish

A lacquer finish should be applied by a professional furniture finisher because special spray equipment is needed. Lacquer has the advantage of being crystal-clear and colorless, but it does not hold up as well as varnish.

Shellac

Shellac should *not* be used as a finish. It is neither durable nor water- and alcohol-proof, and should be employed only as an intermediate coating to protect stenciling against bleeding during the varnishing process, or as an initial sealer on raw wood.

Preparation of floors

Old finishes must be removed from a floor by machine sanding before it is prepared for stenciling. Even a new floor must be sanded smooth before anything can be done to it, and old floors have accumulations of wax, paint, varnish, and dirt that must be removed before new finishes can be successfully applied. Most people will prefer to have their floors sanded professionally, since it requires a certain amount of skill and is tiring work. Caution the floor sander, however; the floor should not be overdone with fine sandpaper, because doing so produces a shiny surface that does not take stain or paint well.

Always vacuum a floor after sanding, and go over it with a tack cloth to pick up any remaining particles of dust before proceeding to the next step.

Backgrounds for floors

There are several ways to prepare a background for stenciling floors:

Bleaching must be done professionally; it involves the use of strong preparations and some experience. Two bleachings produce a lovely creamy color in an oak floor. One bleaching under a white stain will keep it from having a pinkish cast. A light hand-sanding should follow bleaching because the process raises the grain of the wood.

Staining allows the wood grain to show through the color. Unless the floor has been bleached first, the color of the wood (ranging from beige to orange) will modify the color of the stain. Floors are stained in the same manner as any other wood surface (see page 55).

Glazing, as explained earlier, is the application of a thinned paint coat, usually over a light or white background color (see page 58). The process gives a beautiful depth and luminosity to whatever color you use. A good base for a floor glazing mixture is a penetrating oil sealer. (The glazing of a floor is described in detail in Project 2, p. 106.)

Oil-base paint is the preferred material for applying solid background color to a floor. It can be mixed to order in a variety of colors at good paint stores, or tinted as desired at home with a universal colorant. A flat finish is best, but a satin finish is also acceptable. If the paint is too thick, thin it with turpentine to good brushing consistency. Apply it in sections, following the cracks between floor boards to avoid overlapping, painting with as large a brush as you can handle. A 3″ brush is usually sufficient. Two coats will probably be necessary to produce an adequately opaque color. One coat, if it is even, produces a pleasant, somewhat pickled effect, like that of a stain. The paint must dry at least twenty-four hours before stenciling.

Water-base paints (such as acrylic or latex paints) dry much more rapidly than oil-base paint but raise the grain of the wood, so a light sanding between coats is necessary. Since the sanding takes off some of the paint, at least two coats are required. After the final coat sand very lightly with a very fine production paper. In good drying weather it is possible to apply two coats in one day and be ready to stencil the next. Feel the floor with your hand. If it is cool to the touch, it is probably not dry yet. Any water-base paint, unless it is thoroughly dry, can cause acetate stencils to curl up. Always vacuum and use a tack cloth to pick up dust after even a light sanding. Save some of your ground color for later touch-ups.

Finishing floors

The only coating recommended for use over a stenciled floor is varnish. The newest synthetic varnishes are extremely durable and as easy to apply as any coat of paint. *Polyurethane* is a general name for a whole class of synthetic varnishes; they are also sometimes called *urethanes*. Follow the directions on the can. The best way to apply any varnish is with a brush. However, if you are in a hurry and do not object to a slight pebbliness in the surface, varnish may be applied with a roller. Follow the same preparations and precautions recommended for varnishing furniture (page 59).

Turpentine is the usual solvent for varnish and is used to thin the first coat slightly and to clean brushes. Mineral spirits may be substituted for turpentine for brush cleaning.

All varnishes add some color of their own to the floor, usually yellowish or amber, and sometimes beige. Never expect a painted floor to look pure white when it has been varnished. The best way to preview the final effect is to make a test on a piece of wood of everything you will use, from preparation through stenciling to the final finish. This will also show whether any of the colors will bleed, and provide advance notice of any other special problems. If you have not made such a sample, test the varnish on an unobtrusive corner of the floor before going ahead with the varnishing. Let the varnish dry for an hour and examine the stenciling for bleeding. One or more days' extra drying time are sometimes necessary for pigments (such as reds) that bleed readily. If they still run, apply a thin coat of shellac to isolate the stenciling, and then varnish.

Keep the room well-ventilated when using these preparations; the fumes can be toxic.

Lacquer preparations are not recommended for use over stenciled floors because their base is a powerful volatile solvent.

Wax, although it provides an extremely hard finish when properly buffed, is not recommended because it requires constant renewal to protect a stenciled floor; its slick finish prevents the application or re-application of varnish, and it cannot be removed or replaced without also dissolving the stenciling.

Preparing and finishing tinware

Tinware may be successfully stenciled, provided its surface is not so elaborately curved that paint will run under the stencil. Some examples of toleware designs can be adapted to stencils.

Bronze powder stenciling effects may also be executed with acetate stencils and gold or silver paint (see page 91).

If the tin is old and shows rust spots, go over it with a rust remover. Wash the tin with soap and water and dry *thoroughly*. Sand it smooth with a fine sandpaper if necessary. On both old and new tin, apply a metal primer. Let it dry for twenty-four hours. The primer protects the tin from future rust. Paint the tinware with a flat oil-base paint, being careful to minimize brushstrokes. One or two coats will provide a good surface for your stenciling. After the customary generous drying time of from three days to a week, protect the stenciling with two coats of varnish, applying it as you would on any other japan paint stenciling.

Superimposing design shapes to produce additional tones or colors.

8. Color

The doors and windows of your color imagination are waiting to be opened. Nature is the perfect place to look for the sources of inspiration that will release them; it is never wrong where color is concerned. What could be more stimulating than autumn leaves? Look at a bunch of wild grasses or weeds growing in a field. Even when they are peeking through the snow, dried and brittle, they are breathtakingly beautiful. Study the colors of birds, fish, vegetables. Even an ordinary stone can be a wonder of mingled tints and hues. If you are restricted to the city, buy a bouquet of flowers and study their color variations. Go to museums and examine paintings, pottery, jewelry, and furniture. Go to libraries; search out books on Indian and Persian miniatures. Absorb the fantastic colors of an Oriental rug. And don't forget the rich heritage of color design to be found in Early American and European decoration.

Color charts have been intentionally avoided here. Color is a very personal experience, one that touches, in a sense, on the illimitable. Nevertheless, it has to be brought down to earth. Paint must realize the vision in the mind's eye. The colors suggested for stenciling should be thought of only as ingredients for experiment. What you do with them must reflect your individual experience.

For the various Projects presented in this book, we have selected colors we felt were appropriate to them. If something else would please you more, by all means revise the combinations to suit yourself.

Although there are no absolutes that govern color choice, there are some technical observations about the behavior of japan color that should be made.

Artists' oils and color

The virtue of japan paint is its faculty of drying instantaneously. However, the japan medium has a slight brownish cast that tends to dull some colors, especially if white is added or the colors are inter-

mixed. The colors can be made more brilliant by adding a small amount of artists' oil paint to the japan color. Never use more than one part artists' oil paint to four parts japan paint. Greater proportions of oil slow down drying too much. In very hot weather, however, add one or two drops of artists' linseed oil to the japan paint mixture because extreme heat dries the paint mixture too quickly. Do not add the linseed oil if you have already added artists' oil paint.

Some manufacturers offer a wider selection of japan colors than others. But as long as you have the basic colors on hand, plus a few selected artists' oil paints, you will be able to achieve a wide range of beautiful colors.

The basic selection of japan paint colors you need are:

> White (preferably flake white, although striping white and French zinc white are also available in the japan medium)
> Black. Lampblack is preferred; drop black is also available
> Chrome yellow. It comes in Med (medium), L (light), and LL (light light)
> American vermilion L (light)
> American vermilion D (dark)
> Venetian red
> French yellow ochre
> Raw sienna
> Burnt sienna
> Raw umber
> Burnt umber
> Cobalt blue
> Ultramarine blue
> Prussian blue
> Chrome green. Medium (Med) is definitely needed; you may also want dark (dk) and light (L). This color is also called C.P. green

There are no satisfactory pinkish reds or purples available in japan paint. For these and for other colors not obtainable in japan paints, you will have to mix artists' oil colors with the japan medium. The artists' oil colors you need are:

Alizarin crimson
Cobalt violet
Viridian
Cadmium lemon
Prussian blue (optional)
Cadmium red medium
Thalo green (optional)
Manganese violet (optional)
Dioxazine purple

When adding artists' oils to japan colors, always work out the mixture on a saucer or piece of glass with the palette knife until the paints gradually become thoroughly blended.

Juxtaposed colors can change each other. For example, yellow or green will tend to make any blue next to them look lavender. Colors also appear different in artificial light. This is particularly true of fluorescent lighting. The true color is visible in good natural daylight, but direct sunlight changes it. Varnishing over colors makes them more brilliant and intense, but it will also add a slight amber quality. These effects are difficult to foresee. Make color tests before going ahead with any project.

Adding colors by overprinting

A three-color design may be done with only two stencils by printing one color over another. Cut some of the design shapes in *both* stencils, and when you print the second stencil, the second color will print over that of the first stencil, producing a third color. This is a simple process, but you must select the right colors. Yellow printed over blue (or vice versa) may yield several pleasant shades of green, but some combinations produce only a muddy effect when superimposed. Try them out first. Good results have been obtained with yellow and blue to make green, red over white to make pink, and red over yellow to make orange.

Printing in tones of one color

Varied shades may be printed with one color and two stencils. Plan the design so that the shapes in one stencil will overlap those of the other in printing. The many tone variations produced give the design greater depth and delicacy. To control the printing, use only a minimum of paint on your brush.

"Antique" colors

The easiest way to approximate the mellowing of age is to tone down a color by adding a small amount of raw umber. This seems almost too simple, but this pigment has a unique way of aging a color without making it look muddy. Raw umber is highly concentrated, so add very little of it to your mixture.

Handling reds

During varnishing, red tends to bleed more than any other color. This is true of just about every shade of red, even the earthy ones. When you are ready to apply a finish, first isolate and protect the stencil prints with a light coat of shellac.

Stenciling dark on light/light on dark

Most stenciling is executed in dark tones over a light background. To be effective, the background should be a contrasting one, because the stencil paint is applied sparsely and is partly translucent. The degree of contrast can vary, depending on the effect desired.

On a *dark* background it is sometimes necessary to stencil over some of the colors a second time, particularly when the stenciling is done in medium tones of red, blue, or green. If you stencil with white or very pale pastel colors against a dark background, the contrast is easily achieved and the result can be truly lovely.

The effect of drying

Some colors darken as they dry, while others become lighter, depending on such factors as the proportion of white in the mixture. The color of the paint when wet is truer to the final, finished effect than the dry color because the varnish heightens the color, closely restoring it to its appearance when wet.

Beginning students tend to paint with primary colors right out of the can or tube. Released from the classroom to gather wild flowers and grasses, they come back thrilled, not so much at the whole range of colors and color combinations existing in nature as at the discovery that they possess their own color imagination and can visualize subtle, beautiful effects they have never been conscious of before. They are awakened to color as energy capable of affecting sensibility and mood and influencing everything around it.

When you are armed with a few facts about technique, plus *inspiration,* there is no reason that you should not become a truly accomplished colorist.

List of Plates

3

5

4

9

10

11

12

14

13

15

16

17

18

19

20

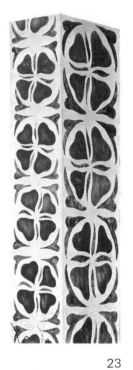

23

24

22

25

26

27

28

29

30

31

32

33

34

35

36

37

42

43

44

45

46

47

48

9. More Ways to Stencil

As you progress beyond the basic techniques of cutting stencils, mixing colors, and handling a brush, you find there is a wide range of possibilities in the ways that stenciling may be used.

Stenciling with a roller

A roller may be used for stenciled designs in which unmodulated solid color is more suitable than the delicate shading of brush stenciling. Many geometric designs fall into this category. Some floral motifs and designs with large, simplified shapes look very well when done with a roller. Good results have been obtained by using a roller on a simple Early American floor design with a motif of large leaves. The principal reason for using the roller is the ease and speed with which it can be used to cover large areas. There is seldom occasion to use one for anything else; brushwork is more subtle and less wasteful of paint.

Cutting stencils for roller work

Larger margins than usual—at least 3″—must be left around the edges on stencils that will be printed by a roller. The shapes should be slightly larger than usual, cut just outside the drawn lines instead of on them. Rollers never fill in the shapes as fully as brushes do, and a gap will appear between adjacent shapes unless you make the stencil openings a little larger. Do not overdo this in the initial cutting; you can always enlarge later.

The stencils should always face in the same direction, especially in doing geometric floors. Mark the word "Top" on each stencil along with its number and/or color. Keep this notation turned toward some landmark in the room—a door, window, or fireplace—and place the successive stencils all in the same way. This will ensure exact registration within the repeat.

Mixing paint for roller work

A much larger quantity of japan paint than usual must be mixed for roller painting. A glass mixing bowl is best, but a paper bucket from the paint store will do. All the colors for the project should be mixed in advance, thinned only enough for easy stirring, and stored in tightly covered containers. A small quantity at a time can be mixed to rolling consistency when you are ready to use it, but the full amount must be prepared initially to keep the color consistent.

Proceed gradually in mixing this large batch of paint, adding color slowly. Save some back for correcting the tone and intensity, and test the color from time to time. To make the test, add a little turpentine to a small quantity of the paint until the paint has a milky consistency. Spread it on a piece of paper or wood to see if the shade is right.

If you must add artists' oil paint to get the right color, take a palette knife and work the oil color into a little of the japan paint on a sheet of glass.

Roller technique

You are ready to print with a roller when the stenciling surface has been marked off into the repeats indicated by the over-all design. The tools and materials needed are:

7″ mohair rollers (on a standard handle)
roller pans
paper buckets or coffee cans (to hold paint)
aluminum foil (to cover paint and wrap rollers)
thick stack of paper towels
cookie sheets with sides
stencils
masking tape
japan paint mixture
turpentine

Working oil color into japan paint.

Arrange these materials on a plastic dropcloth covered with newspaper.

Roller paint should be thin enough so that it fully fills in design shapes without building up a heavy coat on the surface, yet it should be dry enough so that it makes a clean print. Work on each print until it has a good edge. Whether or not a uniform coat is desirable depends on the type of design. A little uneven variation is generally more interesting.

Pour a little paint into the pan and mix it with turpentine to the consistency of light cream. As the roller and stencil gather paint, gradually make the mixture thinner, until it resembles milk rather than cream. Stir this thinned mixture frequently; in the pan it tends to settle.

The mohair roller has a thick, velvety coating. This must be thoroughly and evenly saturated with paint at the beginning. Tilt the pan so that the well-stirred paint coats the inclined surface, and wait for it to drain off. Firmly roll the roller up and down the incline eight or ten times, then crosswise a few times to even out the coating. Roll it firmly on the stack of paper towels in the cookie sheet. If the print you make on these towels is spotty or too dry, saturate the roller again. It should make a solid block of color on the towels. Throw away the top towels when they are wet and start again with the fresh ones underneath. When you have towels showing a solid impression that is no longer very wet but has begun to show a dry texture, try the roller on the floor you are going to stencil. Experiment in an inconspicuous area, perhaps one that will later be hidden by a piece of furniture; tape the stencil down firmly and use the roller lightly at first. With practice and by lifting the edge of the stencil to examine the print, you will soon learn how much paint you can safely carry on the roller to get good results without danger of its running under the stencil. Err on the side of dryness rather than wetness until you get the hang of it. When the paint load is just right, you can print with considerable pressure.

Common sense dictates certain procedures for roller stenciling. The prints of a roller are wetter and thicker than those of a brush, they dry more slowly, and so more care must be taken not to put the stencil down where it will touch a preceding print that is still wet. Plan the printing order so that you skip alternate sections, giving the adjacent ones time to dry; then go back and fill in the spaces in your next trip across the floor. Watch where you step. Wear cotton socks, preferably white, when decorating a floor. This keeps feet and floor clean. If you accidentally step on a print, the socks absorb some of the paint and less of it is tracked around. If you work alone, keep an empty cookie sheet handy to hold the roller while you move the stencil. Floor work goes much more rapidly with two people. One does the rolling only, attending to the condition of the roller and paint; the other moves the stencil and keeps the paint stirred and the paint and paper towels in good supply. More than two people may be an unhelpful crowd in a small room.

Storing and cleaning up

Because a roller applies a thicker coating than a

Dry impression shows need for more paint.

Text impression should be solid but not wet.

brush, the stencil may become loaded with paint more often. Stop and clean the stencil frequently, using newspaper topped with paper towels to absorb the excess. If you stop work for a while or overnight, tightly wrap the roller (but not the handle) in aluminum foil to prevent its drying out. Rollers are extremely hard to clean well enough to use again, especially for another color. If possible, consider them expendable; save the handle and throw the roller away when the job is done.

Stenciling on leather

This relatively unexplored technique has great potential. Ideally, one should use authentic leather dyes in stenciling leather. The dyes come in a range of handsome colors and are far more permanent than japan paint. The fumes are hazardous to breathe, but the dye dries as quickly as japan paint and does not mat down the nap on suede the way paint does. Leather dyes and their solvents can be used with all stencil materials.

Stenciling on fabric

Fabric, if it is to be laundered, should be stenciled with textile paints, following the manufacturer's instructions on how to use them. Textile paints are compatible with the acetate stencil. Fabric has a tendency to stretch diagonally during stenciling. Stretch the fabric taut and anchor it securely with thumbtacks on a piece of plywood or masonite. Cotton canvas, duck, or sailcloth, and artists' canvas take to stenciling very well because they are not too heavily textured and do not stretch easily. A heavy grade of canvas, stenciled and well var-

nished, makes a fine floor cloth which may be swept or mopped.

Stenciling with acrylic paint

Acrylic paint may be used for stenciling, provided it is an artists' quality paint and is used with vinyl or Mylar stencils. Unlike the soft variations of japan colors, acrylic paints provide either a solid, opaque color or a transparent or wash-like effect. For contemporary designs that call for unmodulated color application, acrylic paints are satisfactory, and are available in a wide range of colors.

Although the actual stenciling technique is the same, acrylic paint forms a skin as it dries, so frequent rinsings of the brush are necessary to keep the bristles flexible. Brushes are cleaned and the paint is thinned with water. Keep containers of water handy, and squeeze the excess water from the brush with clean, dry tissues each time it is rinsed.

Designs are traced onto the stencils with a technical drawing pen and India ink for cutting, but because the paint is thinned with water, the stencils cannot be registered with ink, which is also water-soluble. Notches must be used instead.

To clean the skin of paint that forms on the stencils, use a moistened pad of steel wool. Wipe the stencil gently and firmly and remove the residue with moistened tissues. Dry the stencil between two paper towels and press it flat under a weighted piece of glass.

Stenciling with gold or silver paint

Stenciling in metallic colors is done in the same way as with japan paint. Ready-mixed metallic

91

Using a corner guide to print cards in quantity.

Card is placed in corner with first stencil hinged to table.

paints do not dry fast enough for stenciling, so you must mix your own. Using a palette knife and glass, mix equal amounts of metallic powder with a fast-drying flat varnish. In place of turpentine, thin the mixture with lighter fluid or cleaning fluid. (These fluids are flammable and toxic; don't smoke, keep the window open, and avoid inhaling the fumes as you work.) The paint consistency should be that of soft butter.

Sponge or velour technique

To add a stylized texture to stencil prints, a sponge or piece of velour may be substituted for the stencil brush. Experiment to see whether stippling or stroking the paint onto the surface looks better. Always remove surplus paint from the sponge or velour before stenciling.

Printing with paper stencils

When you are working with simple designs that are repeated over a large area, multiple paper stencils can be very useful for cutting down stenciling time. Identical stencils can be taped together end-to-end to speed the printing of a long border, or joined together in a square to do several repeats of an all-

over pattern at one time. Paper stencils wear out rapidly; it is wise to have more than one if they are to be used repeatedly. Extra stencils also make it possible for several people to work together on large surfaces such as floors or walls. This time-saving technique works best for simple designs that can be executed with only one stencil.

1. Trace the design for each stencil onto a piece of tracing paper the same size as the proposed stencil.
2. Stack two, three, or four sheets of stencil paper on your cutting surface. (More than four would be difficult to cut accurately.) Be sure all the sheets are exactly the same size. Place the traced design on top.
3. Tape the stack together on all four sides with masking tape to keep the sheets from shifting.
4. Following the traced design, cut through the stack with a sharp blade. Bear down hard to cut through all the layers. Remove the tape and you have four stencils, all exactly the same, and the

Card is moved to next corner to print second stencil.

Separate corners may be used for each stencil.

stenciling may proceed at a very rapid pace.

Printing cards and posters

To print large numbers of greeting cards, place mats, posters, or similar flat items with a design that requires accurate registration, construct two or more square corner guides with pieces of heavy cardboard. As many corners can be used as you have stencils, with one person printing at each one. For example, to print a greeting card from three stencils, already cut with uniform borders and with accurate register marks:

1. Cut two short lengths of cardboard for each stencil (a total of six in this case). Make sure that the inner edge is perfectly straight.
2. Tape two strips down firmly at right angles on your work surface. Use a draftsmen's right-angle triangle to place them, or, lacking this, use one of the greeting cards as a guide. Space the other corners along the table to give each stenciler room.

3. Push a card firmly up into the first corner. Place Stencil 1 over it in position. Tape the stencil securely to the table along one edge so that it is, in effect, *hinged* to the table. Print.
4. Raise the stencil, take out the card, and move it to the second corner. Push it in firmly. Place Stencil 2 accurately over the card and tape it in place as you did the first. Print it, and correct its position, if necessary, in relation to the print made by the first stencil.
5. Repeat the entire procedure with the third corner and Stencil 3. When the final print is correctly placed, leave the stencils hinged in position and proceed with printing all the cards.

With one person in charge of each corner and one stencil, and each stenciler inserting a card, flipping down the stencil onto it, printing, removing the card, and handing it to the next person, you have an effective assembly line in operation, ready to turn out hundreds of cards or posters in an afternoon.

10. Projects

These eight projects have been selected and arranged in order of increasing complexity, based on the length of time it takes to execute them, the stenciling technique required, and the number of stencils involved.

Once you have become acquainted with the tools and techniques of stenciling, you will not find these projects difficult, especially if you have tried some of the practice designs given in Chapter 4.

Each project includes all the specific information necessary for its completion, including materials, the way to prepare the stencils, how to plan, measure, and lay out the design, and the particular stenciling technique to be used. The preparation and finishing of the surface are explained, and the average time needed to complete the stenciling is also noted so that you won't face unexpected pressures as you progress.

Any additional materials required beyond the usual ones—stencils, japan paint, turpentine, stenciling brushes, and drawing, tracing, and measuring equipment—are listed at the beginning of each project. Recipes and ingredients for mixing the stenciling colors and the various background and finishing preparations are given individually with the instructions for those procedures.

All the designs are presented in usable sizes and may be traced directly from the book. They may be enlarged or reduced to fit the dimensions of the article you are decorating by following the directions in Chapter 11. The designs can be applied to other articles, and the colors changed to suit your need.

The Plate number given at the beginning of each project refers to the color photograph that shows the finished design. In the designs to be traced, separate gray tones and textured patterns indicate the different colors. The palest tone of gray shows where the repetitions of a design meet.

If you wish to avoid becoming tired mentally or physically, five hours of concentrated work per day is about all you should expect to be able to do.

Project 1

Mirror frame, window shade, stool, and small chest

The designs used on these four articles employ simple procedures frequently used in stenciling and present an opportunity to try out different kinds of backgrounds. All would adapt well to any number of projects.

The *mirror frame* design is printed in two colors with only one stencil. The *window shade* shows how to use two stencils for one color by superimposing them. The *stool* is an exercise in squaring off an all-over repeat design to fit a specific object. The *small chest* brings together several individual designs on one piece.

Mirror Frame

(*Plate 35, page 78*)
1 stencil, 2 colors

This design may be printed in total, or in part if the frame is not wide enough to hold the whole design. By blocking out parts of the design in the first printing, the single stencil may be used to print two colors. The background color is made more interesting by using a glaze over it.

Time
1. Preparing the surface with gesso: half a day, including drying time. Apply glaze the following morning.
2. Tracing and cutting the stencil (while glaze is drying): from two to three hours; less if you are experienced.
3. Printing the design on the frame: half a day maximum.
   Total: one day, plus about three days to dry and five minutes for varnishing.

Additional materials
Gesso, glaze, shellac (optional), varnish.

Preparing the surface
Apply two coats of gesso to give the frame a moderately textured surface. When the gesso is completely dry, apply a yellow glaze prepared by the formula given in Chapter 7, adding to it:

> 1 teaspoon chrome yellow medium japan
>   paint
> ¼ teaspoon yellow ochre japan paint

Mirror frame design. Both colors may be printed from a single stencil.

Allow the glaze to dry thoroughly (at least three hours) before stenciling.

Preparing the stencil

Prepare a single stencil of the entire design, allowing a 1″ margin all around. Put placement marks at the end of the stencil. Make a few proofs on paper.

Measuring and marking

Guidelines are unnecessary—follow the edge of the frame. To space the design evenly around the frame, arrange the paper proofs along it and mark their position so the stencil can be placed accordingly. The full stencil is used only on the broad base of the mirror; the sides and top are decorated only with the elements of the design that will gracefully fit the narrower space.

Stenciling

1. Green is the predominant color here; stencil the green elements of the design first over the entire frame. Block out those shapes that are to be stenciled in red. For the green, prepare:

    1 teaspoon chrome green light japan paint

    When all the green is printed, remove the tape and clean the stencil thoroughly.
2. Replace the clean stencil over the design. Frame the parts that are to be printed in red with small pieces of masking tape. Print all the red parts of the design, using:

    1 teaspoon American vermilion light japan paint

Take care that the brush does not go beyond the area isolated with tape. Remove the tape carefully before cleaning the stencil.

Finishing

When dry, the stenciling may be finished with flat or satin varnish. Test the red paint first, and if it shows a tendency to bleed, isolate the stenciling with shellac before varnishing.

Printing the first color. Block out red while stenciling green.

Printing the second color. Frame red shapes with tape to prevent smudging.

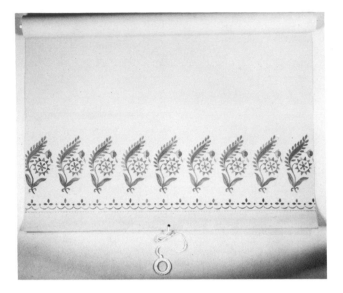

Window Shade

(Plate 15, page 72)
2 stencils, 1 color

This is the simplest of projects; window shades need no surface preparation or final finish. A variety of attractive colors is available, but avoid slick materials. Here we have chosen a cloth shade with a warm tan background. The design is printed in only one color, but two stencils are used with varied printing impressions to produce an effect of two tones of green.

Time

1. Tracing and cutting stencils: half a day. Measuring and marking off is done while you are stenciling.
2. Printing: about an hour.
3. Clean-up: half an hour.
   Total: five hours or less.

Additional materials
None.

Preparing the stencils

Make two stencils and include register and placement marks as you trace the design. The two tones of green are shown here as black and gray; this is your guide to the division of the color onto the two stencils. Make a number of proofs on paper; use them to plan the arrangement of the design on the shade.

Measuring and marking off

Utilize the hem of the shade as a guideline to keep the design running straight. Avoid making pencil marks; erasing leaves marks on the shade. Proper placement of the design usually can be calculated by using the paper proofs.

Stenciling
Mix:

> 1 teaspoon chrome green light japan paint
> $\frac{1}{8}$ teaspoon raw umber japan paint

1. Place the first stencil in position. Print it quite pale. Keep the same degree of paleness in each print. Complete the row with the first stencil.
2. Place the second stencil in position, following register marks for placement. As you print the second stencil, use greater pressure on the brush to achieve a darker tone, but do not exaggerate. Keep your fingers clean as you work; paint and oil smudges are difficult to remove from cloth shades.

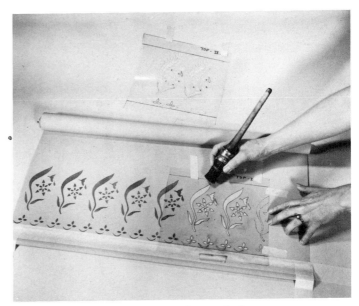

Printing the first stencil. A light touch keeps prints evenly pale in tone.

Printing the second stencil. Greater pressure makes a darker print.

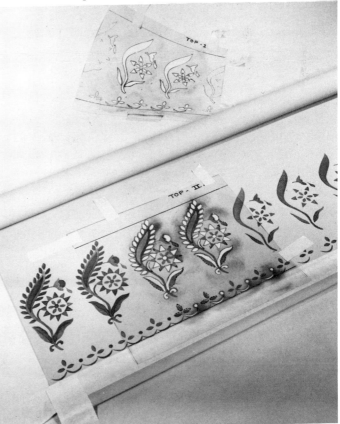

Stool

(*Plate 14, page 72*)
2 stencils, 1 color

The design on this small stool, printed in blue on a white background, features an all-over repeat with a matching border.

Time
1. Preparation of the surface: half a day. Stencils are prepared while the gesso is drying.
2. Measuring and marking the surface: one hour maximum.
3. Stenciling: about half a day.
   Total: one and a half days, plus three days to dry and about five minutes to varnish.

Additional materials
Gesso, gloss varnish.

Preparing the stencils
Accurate measuring and marking are important for this all-over design. Each time the stencil is printed the design must fit the adjacent print exactly so that no separation is visible. As you trace the design, make guidelines on the stencil to correlate with the squares that will be marked off on the surface, and placement marks to help connect the design sections. Cut separate stencils for the border (below) and for the all-over repeat (page 102).

Preparing the surface
Apply two coats of gesso (or white paint). When it is completely dry, sand the gesso smooth. The stenciling is done directly on the gesso.

Measuring and marking
Mark off a 1½″ border all around the edge of the stool. Beginning from the center, mark off the remaining surface in squares the same size as those on the stencil, checking accuracy with a triangle. Draw the lines very lightly in pencil so they may be easily erased. Because of the proportions of the stool, the only complete representation of the design falls in its center.

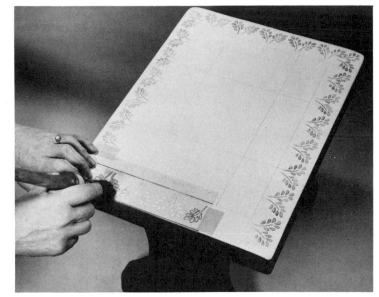

Printing the border.

Stenciling

1. Begin with the border design. Mix japan paint:
       1 teaspoon white
       1/2 teaspoon ultramarine blue
   Make paper proofs and use them to plan the arrangement of the border at the corners. Using the guidelines, line up the stencil with the penciled lines on the stool. Print the border on all four sides.

2. Mask off the border area with strips of masking tape. Place the stencil of the all-over design in the center square marked on the stool.

3. Following the guidelines, print the design in all the squares until the surface is completely decorated. Remove the masking tape protecting the border. Allow the paint to dry thoroughly before removing the pencil marks with a kneaded eraser.

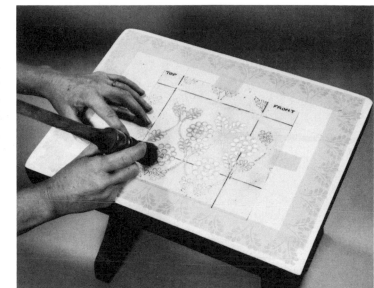

Printing the center square.

Completing the all-over design.

Finishing

When the stenciling is thoroughly dry, varnish over it with a high gloss or satin-finish varnish. Two coats are usually sufficient.

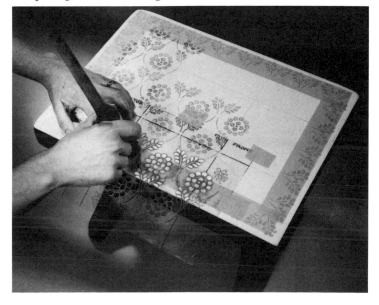

Small Chest

(Plate 13, page 72)
4 stencils, 2 colors

Combining a few very simple designs in two different colors produces an attractive effect. Printing the
design in lighter colors than that of the background
helps to enrich the scheme. The colors selected for
the stenciling should be of about the same intensity,
so that one does not overpower the other. Brass
handles and a key plate purchased from a hardware store add a touch of elegance, and an historic
date or monogrammed letters applied from pre-cut,
store-bought stencils make the chest a conversation
piece.

Time
1. Preparing the surface: three days, allowing ample drying time between coats of gesso, paint,
   and glaze.
2. Cutting and making paper stencils: done while
   the surface preparations are drying. Tracing and
   cutting takes three or four hours.
3. Measuring and marking the surface: may add
   half an hour to the stenciling time.
   Total: one-half to one full day, plus drying time
   and about five minutes to varnish.

Additional materials
Gesso, glaze, varnish, brass hardware.

Preparing the surface
1. Apply one or two coats of gesso; sand lightly
   when dry.
2. Paint the background with a japan paint mixture of:

      1 tablespoon white
      1 tablespoon Prussian blue
      ½ teaspoon raw umber

   If necessary, increase the amount of paint. Thin
   it well with turpentine.

Scallop stencil is reversed to form border ovals.

Flowers are spaced to leave room for border vine.

3. Protect the background with a coat of varnish *before* the glaze is applied.
4. For the glaze color, which will be darker than that of the background, use the same proportions of white and Prussian blue, but double the amount of raw umber to 1 teaspoon and mix, following the glaze formula given in Chapter 7. Let the glaze dry before stenciling.

Preparing the stencils
Allow a 1″ margin around the design on all your stencils, making one each for the scallop, the vine, the flowers, and the base border.

Measuring and marking
Experiment with paper proofs to determine the placement. If possible, arrange the borders so they come out evenly on both ends. Center the flower design on the front and ends of the chest. Don't crowd the designs; the spacing between them and the borders is aesthetically important.

Stenciling
1. Stencil the scallop design on all edges except around the base. Mix the apricot color, using:

> 1 teaspoon white japan paint
> ½ teaspoon chrome yellow medium japan paint
> ⅛ teaspoon alizarin crimson artists' oil paint

Stir well. Turn the scallop around to form ovals at the edges of the chest.
2. Print the flower design in apricot on the front and sides of the chest, leaving ample space for the vine. Mix the mint green for the vine in the following proportions of japan paint:

> 1 teaspoon white
> ½ teaspoon chrome green light
> ⅛ teaspoon ultramarine blue

3. Arrange the vine border around the front and sides of the chest so it comes out evenly, and stencil it, leaving a pleasing space between vine and flowers.

4. Print the green vine on the top of the chest, blocking off unneeded shapes at the end with tape. Make a rectangle large enough to accommodate comfortably a monogram or date stenciled in apricot.

5. Print the monogram or date.

6. In mint green, stencil the base border all around the bottom molding. Any minor mistakes may be easily removed as you go along because the chest was glazed before stenciling. Dry at least three days before varnishing.

Finishing

Apply two coats of satin varnish. Add a coat of clear Butcher's Wax and rub it to a handsome finish with a fine steel wool (#000). Drill holes for the keyhole and handles, and attach the hardware.

ABOVE: the vine is placed parallel to the edges of the chest.

BELOW: placement marks connect prints and unneeded repeats are blocked off with tape.

Project 2

Japanese floral floor design

(Plate 48, page 88)
4 stencils, 1 color

Derived from an old Japanese stencil, this floral design is executed in colors that might have been used with the original. The floor is glazed a deep indigo blue over a white background, and the stencils are all printed in white.

The amounts of paint suggested and the time needed for completion of the work are sufficient for a floor not much bigger than 15′ × 15′.

Time

1. Preparation of the floor after sanding: three days, including undercoat, sanding, glazing, and one day of drying.
2. Preparing the stencils: several hours, done while the floor is drying.
3. Printing: one to three days, depending on proficiency.
4. Drying: three days.
5. Varnishing: a few hours on two successive days, plus at least one day's drying time.
   Total: nine to twelve days over-all.

Additional materials

One quart flat white oil-base paint, two 3″ brushes, one gallon penetrating oil sealer, #120 Production paper, proof paper, one gallon polyurethane varnish.

Preparing the surface

Have the floor sanded. Go over it with a vacuum cleaner and tack cloth, picking up all dust.

With a broad brush, apply a full and even coat of flat white oil-base paint thinned with turpentine to good brushing consistency. The wood should be almost completely covered by one coat. If the paint soaks in too much, leaving the floor dark, apply another coat the next day.

After a full day's drying, run quickly and lightly over the floor with the sandpaper to remove any roughness. Vacuum and use tack cloth.

Mix a japan-paint glaze consisting of:

> 8 parts ultramarine blue
> 3 parts Prussian blue
> 2 parts raw umber

Use enough to make about one quart of japan color and add it to:

> 1 gallon penetrating oil sealer

Combine and stir well. The blue tends to settle, so stir the glaze frequently as you paint. Flow it onto the floor with a fairly full brush, and go back over your strokes as little as possible. The coating does not have to be perfectly even, and brushstrokes may be allowed to show. Follow the direction of the floor boards, avoiding dark overlaps. Allow to dry for at least one day.

Preparing the stencils

Cut the stencils with a good 2″ border all around the designs. Proofs may be made on any sort of paper, including brown wrapping paper, but they will give the best results printed on paper close in color to that of the painted floor. Make as many proofs of each of the designs as time and paper allow.

Open foldouts. ►

Placement

Use the proofs to arrange the design on the floor. If you have enough proofs, you can lay out the whole floor at once. If not, arrange and print one area at a time. Scatter the proofs at random, turning them in different directions for variety.

1

Stenciling

Flake white japan paint straight from the can or tube is mixed in small amounts with turpentine for printing this floor. When you are ready to print, place each of the stencils over its proof, slip the proof out from beneath it, and print. The print may be fairly faint or transparent, since a blush of blue showing through enhances white. Allow at least three days' drying time before varnishing.

2

Finishing

Apply polyurethane varnish following instructions given in Chapter 7.

This design looks well in a great variety of color combinations, such as black on white or bright yellow, or navy on deep red. The background color, instead of being a glaze, might be a solid paint coat, a light stain, or even natural wood. The same design in a somewhat reduced scale would also be appropriate for furniture, fabrics, window shades, or other decorative accessories.

3

1 and 2. Using proofs to place the design.

3 and 4. A light touch produces a delicately shaded print.

4

111

113

Project 3

Tile Dado

(*Plate 7, page 68*)
4 stencils, 2 colors

The matching border and delicate blue background of this design help to create the illusion of a real tile dado. The upper part of the walls is painted white. High-gloss varnish applied in two coats over the stenciling imitates the luster of a ceramic glaze and makes the dado scrubbable. The final touch is the application of gray lines between the tiles to simulate grout.

Time
1. Preparation of surface: three to four hours.
2. Measuring and marking off tiles and border: two to three hours.
3. Printing the stencils: two to three days per wall.
4. Drying: three days.
5. Varnishing, done on two consecutive days: one to two hours for each coat.

6. Making the grout lines: one to one-and-a-half hours per wall.
   Total: fifteen to seventeen days, including the extended periods of time needed for the background and finishing preparations to dry between procedures.

Additional materials
Metal yardstick, plumb line, one roll extra-wide masking tape, one quart white latex paint tinted with Universal Colorant, one quart high-gloss varnish, two or three Magic Markers in warm gray #3.

Measuring and marking the dado
Using a sharp pencil and metal yardstick, draw a horizontal line from one end of the wall to the other, measuring upward exactly 27¼″ from the

Yellow
Green

Stencil yellow portion of border first.

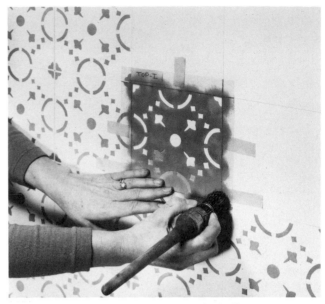

Yellow tiles are printed in marked-off squares.

baseboard (not the floor) on all the walls. Draw the lines very lightly so they won't need to be erased.

Painting in the dado

To establish a clean, sharp, painted edge along the top of the dado, apply strips of wide masking tape above the horizontal pencil line. Use tape to protect baseboard, window sash, or other moldings from the paint. The background color should be very pale, just off white. Have the latex paint tinted when you buy it, or tint it yourself with a drop or two of ultramarine blue Universal Colorant. Mix well. Mix enough paint for all the dadoes and a little extra for touching up. If the latex paint is applied with a regular house painter's brush instead of a roller, it will be much smoother and make the tile design look as if the dadoes were really tiled. Allow the latex paint to dry overnight.

Marking off for the tiles and border

To mark the border, draw another horizontal line exactly 3¼″ below the top of the dado from one end of each wall to the other. Keep the pencil lines light. Now measure and mark off four more horizontal lines below the border from one end of each wall to the other and exactly 6″ apart.

Mark *vertical* lines every 6″ all around the dado. The tiles are 6″ × 6″ squares. Make the first vertical line at the end of the wall that is the most conspicuous. Then, if the dimensions of your wall make it necessary to print only half a tile, it will be less obvious. If the walls are not entirely straight, use a plumb line to assure a more accurate placement of the lines.

Preparing the stencils

Both the tile and the border design are printed in two colors. You will need a stencil for each color. Trace the stencil for the yellow part of the tile first. Be sure to draw the outline of the square on the stencil accurately—it must correlate with the squares marked off on the dado. To avoid confusion, mark the stencils by sequence number and color: #1 (yellow) and #2 (green).

Trace the green stencil, making register marks to insure accurate printing.

Trace the stencils for the border design. Speed the work by putting two border tiles on one stencil. Note that in both the tile and border the design shapes fall slightly short of the tile outline, leaving space for the grout line. Remember to mark "top" on all your stencils so they will not be mistakenly printed upside down.

Stenciling

Put your materials on a tray so you can move them around with you. Mix enough japan paint to stencil all the walls. Store the paint mixture in jars, cover them with plastic wrap, and keep them in your freezer to prevent drying out between work sessions.

For the yellow japan paint, mix:

> 2 tablespoons chrome yellow light
> 2 tablespoons golden ochre

The formula for the green japan paint is:

> 2½ tablespoons chrome green light
> 1½ tablespoons white

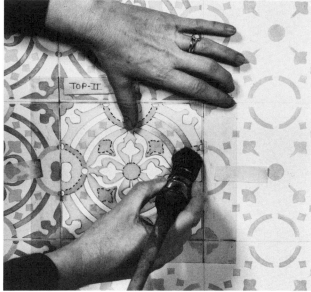

Register marks guide green prints.

After varnish, "grout" lines are added.

The yellow and green should be of about the same intensity so that one does not overpower the other.

Print all the yellow first, putting enough of the mixture in a saucer to stencil one of the walls at a time.

1. Beginning with the border, place the first stencil (yellow) in the marked-off upper section of the dado. Complete the border row in yellow.
2. Place the yellow tile stencil in one of the marked-off 6" squares. Stencil it and continue to print all the yellow within the squares.

    If you have problems fitting the stencil against moldings or baseboard, try one of the solutions given in Chapter 6. If the stencils become clogged with paint, stop and clean them.

    Painting all the yellow first is efficient but monotonous. You may prefer to complete only one wall in yellow before going on to the green, and then start again on the second wall with yellow.
3. When you are ready to print the green, start with the border. Follow the register marks for position—do not rely on the outline of the tile for placement.

Print the entire border in green, and proceed with the stencil for the green tiles, relying on register marks for placement.

Clean the stencil and brush occasionally as you work along the row. Save any unused paint in a small jar. When one wall is completed, clean your stencils and brushes and set aside your materials until you are ready to work on the next one. Allow

a minimum of three days' drying time before varnishing.

Finishing

Make any necessary corrections and do any necessary touching up before you varnish. The grout lines are added *after* the varnish.

Put masking tape above the dado to keep the varnish off the white wall. Using a 3" house painter's brush, give the dadoes an even coat of clear polyurethane high-gloss varnish, stroking away from the masking tape to prevent running under. Move an extra lamp into the room to locate any missed spots. The following day apply a second coat of high-gloss varnish. Wait a day before doing the grout lines.

Grout lines are made with the gray Magic Marker. You will need at least two markers for the four walls. For a more realistic appearance, draw the grout lines for each tile individually. Use a metal ruler as a guide and turn the felt tip from time to time to give some variety to the lines. The ink in this liner is indelible, so there is no need to worry about the grout lines vanishing if you clean the dado with soap and water.

The dado might be executed in two shades of blue, as in Delft tiles, or in blue and mustard yellow, and could be made lower or higher by printing more or fewer rows. Enlarged or reduced, the design is adaptable to table tops and other articles.

Project 4

Tapa coffee table

(Plate 38, page 80)
5 to 15 stencils, 1 color

Micronesian tapa cloth inspired this design printed in black on a faintly antiqued white gesso background. The appearance of hand-painted tapa is simulated by making small irregularities in the stencils and by cutting each one more than once, in slightly varying sizes. The stencils are placed somewhat imprecisely to increase the informal effect, and are printed with more than usual variation.

The table, a standard type provided by makers of unfinished furniture, measures 48″ long, 18″ wide, and stands 18″ high.

Time
1. Preparation of surface: about an hour each on two successive days to gesso, dry, sand lightly, and re-gesso; plus another day's drying, with an hour to sand again and antique the gesso, followed by one day for antiquing to dry thoroughly, or four days in all.
2. Preparation of stencils: about thirty minutes, done while the antiquing dries.
3. Stenciling: about four hours for careful placement and printing, plus at least three days' drying time.
4. Finishing: one hour for varnishing.
   Total: eight hours' work spread over six or seven days.

Additional materials
One pint satin-finish varnish, one pint gesso, antiquing mixture.

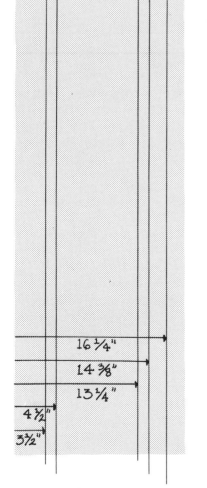

16¼″
14⅜″
13¼″
4½″
3½″

The design arrangement.

Sawtooth, rope, and large triangles. See pages 123 and 124 for additional designs.

Preparing the surface

Brush on two coats of gesso rather roughly. Allow each coat to dry for a day and sand it with #120 Production paper.

Apply a very light antiquing mixture of:

$\frac{3}{4}$ teaspoon black japan paint
$\frac{1}{4}$ teaspoon raw umber japan paint
$\frac{3}{4}$ cup turpentine

Allow the antiquing to dry overnight.

Draw a few light pencil lines on the table top to keep the designs more or less in line, but place the stencils primarily by eye. Starting from the left side and measuring each time *from the left edge,* make marks at points $3\frac{1}{2}''$, $4\frac{1}{2}''$, $13\frac{1}{4}''$, $14\frac{3}{8}''$, and $16\frac{1}{4}''$ from the starting point. Use these marks to draw lines the full length of the table.

Preparing the stencils

Place acetate over each of the designs and trace roughly, leaving at least a 1″ margin. Make two or more stencils of each shape, adding slightly different irregularities to all of them. Make the rectangular blocks in several different lengths, shortening the 6″ size to $5\frac{3}{4}''$ and $5\frac{3}{8}''$ as well as using the full pattern, thus creating a pleasant variation in the prints. When tracing the sawtooth motif, make the stencil double the length shown, so an entire table leg can be stenciled at one time.

Stenciling

Use lampblack or black japan paint straight from the can or tube, mixed as usual with turpentine to printing consistency. To place the designs, follow the diagram. Print them in the following order:

120

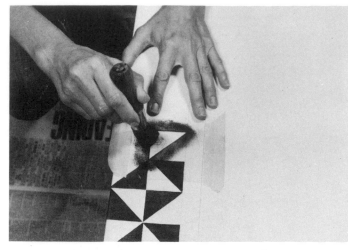

1. Print the pinwheel arrangements in the areas shown in the diagram by turning the stencil for the small triangle in four different directions.

4. To make the narrow black strips, block off part of the large rectangle with a sheet of cardboard.

2. Using the same stencil, make an alternating line of small triangles along the right-hand side of the table top.

5. Print the large triangles, starting from the pinwheels at the top. Gradually fit them in, working across the top and building toward the opposite end. Don't worry if the arrangement is somewhat uneven.

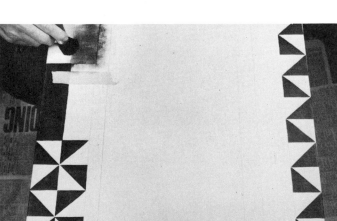

3. Start the rows of rectangular blocks above the pinwheels, alternating them with white ones until you reach the opposite end. Always abut blocks of the same size, but vary the sizes from set to set.

6. Use cardboard to block off part of the triangle where it meets the space left for the rectangular blocks.

7. Insert rectangular blocks at the ends of the rows of large triangles, making them as long as necessary to fill out the space.

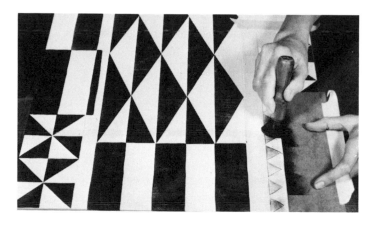

8. The sawtooth row is printed along the line drawn 14⅜″ from the left side of the table, as shown in the first diagram. Half the stencil is covered by cardboard to make a single row of teeth.

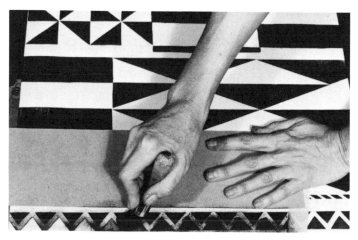

9. Fit the second row of teeth into the first, spacing them by eye. As before, half the stencil is covered by cardboard.

10. Print the tiny rope from one end of the table to the other, spacing it between the sawteeth and the big triangles, and about $\frac{1}{8}''$ from the large triangles. Run all the designs down the apron at the ends and sides of the table.

11. Place the sawtooth stencil in the center of each table leg, starting at the bottom edge of the apron. Print it on all four sides of each leg or just on the two outer edges.

Finishing
Allow at least three days' drying time, then make a test to be sure the black will not bleed during varnishing and require isolating with shellac. If it seems safe, finish with satin-finish varnish.

Project 5

Early American floor and wall design

(Plate 47, page 88)
12 stencils, 2 colors

All the designs included in this project are derived from Early American sources. The colors—dark green and cinnamon—resemble those of their original counterparts. The plaster walls were painted a very pale cream and the old wide-board floor an off-white. The same stencils were used to decorate the walls and to simulate a rug on the floor. Work on the floor was speeded by using a roller in tinting the background of the broad border; the narrow stripe was stenciled with the aid of long strips of acetate.

Time
1. Preparation of the floor after sanding: at least three days. The wide background stripe in the border can dry while the wall is being stenciled.
2. Preparation of stencils: at least a day, but it can be done while the floor is drying.
3. Printing: four days to a week for both walls and floor, followed by at least three days' drying time.
4. Finishing: walls require no finish; floor takes about three days.
   Total: two weeks over-all should be ample.

Additional materials
One gallon white oil-base paint, one tube raw umber Universal Colorant, paint roller, one gallon satin-finish varnish.

Preparing the floor
Have the floor sanded and clean up all dust. Paint the floor with a white oil-base paint tinted very slightly with raw umber Universal Colorant. As you mix in the umber, remember that the protective coats of varnish will darken the color. Save some of the paint for touch-ups which may be needed later.

Preparing the stencils
You will need sufficient acetate for all the designs—more than the usual amount. The straight vine design must be doubled in length to make the complete stencil; you will need a piece of acetate about 19″ long to accommodate tracing it twice.

Make several proofs of each stencil to use in planning placement on the walls.

Measuring and marking the floor
Divide the "rug" part of the floor into 15″ squares with a 15″ wide border all around it. The size of your room will determine how far from the baseboard the border should be placed. In the room shown on page 125, the outside edge of the border is 7″ from the walls. If the area inside the border will not divide equally into 15″ squares, the crossed garland may be cut at any point. The squares on this floor do not have to be absolutely accurate, because the spaces between the stenciled shapes leave room to maneuver, unlike those in Project 7, where a high degree of accuracy is necessary.

Within the 15″ border, mark off the following spaces with a chalk line, starting from the outside edge:

> 1″ stenciled stripe
> ½″ space
> 2″ narrow border design
> ½″ space
> 10″ tinted background for vine
> 1″ stenciled stripe

Sprig design for wall border.

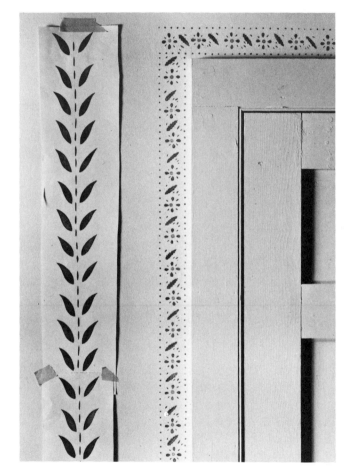

Arrangement of wall frieze.

Preparing the border

If you are going to decorate both wall and floor, color the 10″ section of the floor border first. Use a roller with pieces of acetate to keep the edges straight. Mix japan paint:

>   4 teaspoons white
>   1 drop black
>   1 drop yellow ochre

Add this to:

>   1 pint (or slightly more) turpentine

This mixture produces a very slightly colored turpentine. Do not make it too dark. The roller should be fairly dry as you work; roll out excess paint on paper towels.

Measuring and marking the wall

The frieze at the top of the wall should be placed along a single horizontal guideline 3″ down from the ceiling. The line is made with pencil and yardstick. Make a little mark every $4\frac{1}{2}$″ along it.

Arrange the vertical figured stripes by taping up proofs and shifting them about until a satisfactory distribution is achieved within the dimensions of the room. The presence of windows and doors will affect the spacing. In the room shown, the small border design was used only around the door and windows and along the top of the baseboard; the urns and swags appear only in the paneling under the windows. Avoid overcrowding. Early American craftsmen used sparse decoration to lovely effect.

$4\frac{1}{2}$″

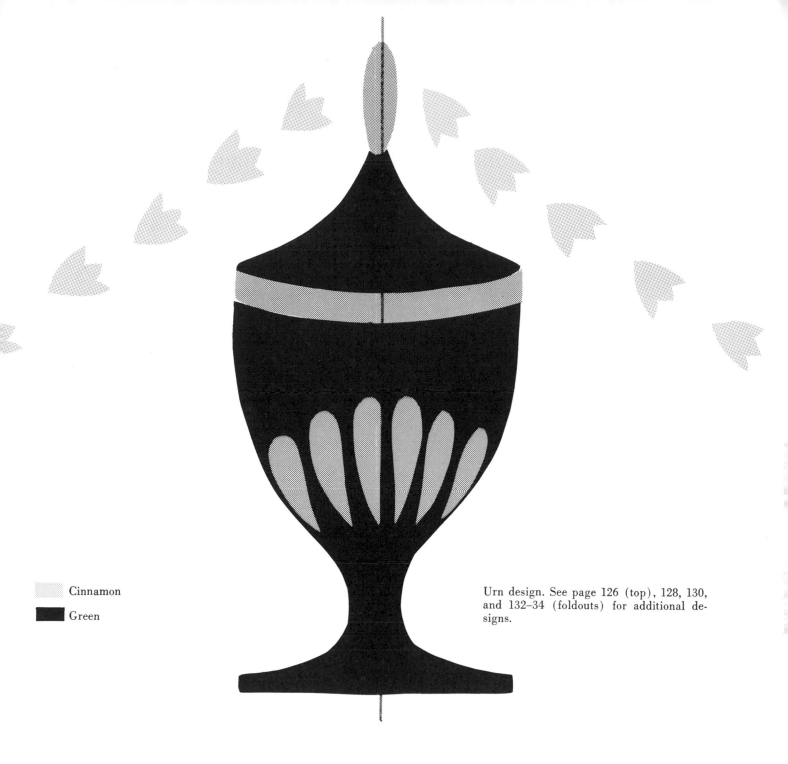

Cinnamon

Green

Urn design. See page 126 (top), 128, 130, and 132–34 (foldouts) for additional designs.

Wherever necessary, use the plumb line to establish vertical guidelines on the wall. Two lines, 10″ apart, are needed for the bird-and-flower vine. Make one center line for the straight vine. The small border design is simply fitted as close as it will go to the windows and door without guidelines.

The little urns were centered on vertical lines 20″ apart. The stencils for the swags between them are designed to be printed twice in that interval, as shown in the illustration inserted above the design for the swag. If the urns cannot be 20″ apart, block off part of the swag to shorten it, or extend it by printing an extra section, but make sure to keep a

nicely flowing curve. The sprig over the swag may be placed by eye, using a proof.

Stenciling the walls
Mix the japan colors for the cinnamon:

> 6 teaspoons yellow ochre light
> 1 teaspoon Venetian red

And for the green:

> 6 teaspoons yellow ochre light
> 1 teaspoon chrome green medium
> 1 scant teaspoon raw umber

Arrangement of urn and swag with flower spray.

The rosette (page 132) and the small sprig (page 126) are printed alternately on the marks made every $4\frac{1}{2}''$ along the top of the wall to form the frieze.

All the two-color designs may be printed either green first or cinnamon first, except for the urns, which must be printed in green first, and the bird-and-flower vine, which must be printed in cinnamon first.

Swag design.

128

◄ Border design

Vine garland ►

Open ►
foldouts

2. Print the straight vine diagonally across the squares between these rosettes as a crossed garland. Space it by eye so that it seems equally distant from the rosettes at either end.

4. Stencil the small border of the "rug." Butt the corners. Using the largest stencil brush you have, add the outer and inner stripes.

3. Where the vine intersects the border, use cardboard or acetate to block out the part that would overlap.

5. Apply both stencils of the bird vine to the tinted section of the border. Printing this vine was saved until last to give the tint maximum drying time.

6. Complete the corners by piecing them out with small design elements extracted from the bird-and-flower vine.

7. Touch up any messy prints with the floor paint set aside for this purpose.

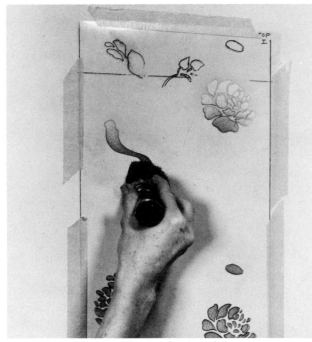

Printing cinnamon birds and flowers.

Adding the green to the vine.

Stenciling the floor

1. Place a rosette at every other crossing of the
   15″ squares, lining up the stencil guidelines
   with those drawn on the floor.

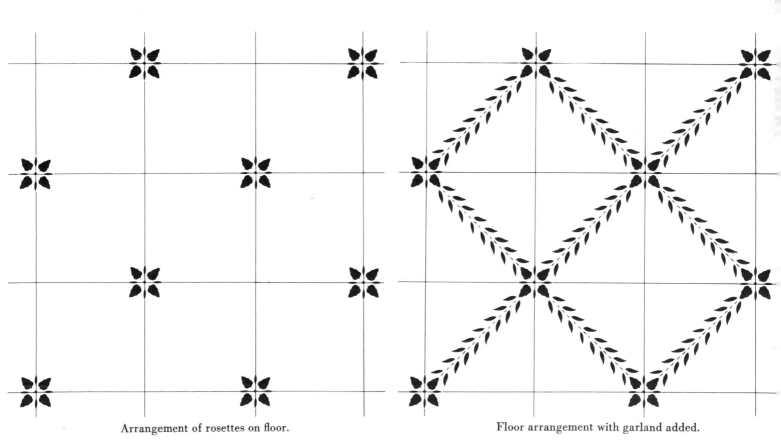

Arrangement of rosettes on floor.

Floor arrangement with garland added.

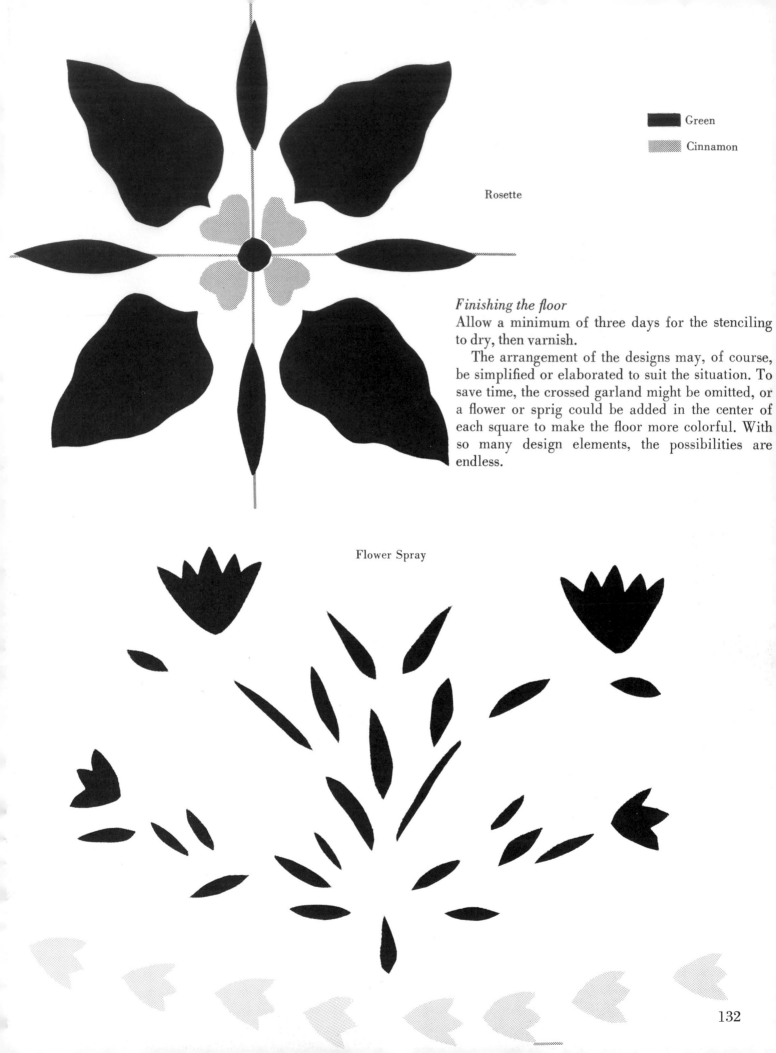

Rosette

Finishing the floor

Allow a minimum of three days for the stenciling to dry, then varnish.

The arrangement of the designs may, of course, be simplified or elaborated to suit the situation. To save time, the crossed garland might be omitted, or a flower or sprig could be added in the center of each square to make the floor more colorful. With so many design elements, the possibilities are endless.

Flower Spray

Time

1. To fill original drawer pull holes, to lightly sand the chest, and to apply two coats of gesso and an antique glaze: two days.
2. Preparing the stencils: about one day.
3. Stenciling: two to three days.
4. Drying time before varnishing: a minimum of three days.
5. Finishing, including coating with shellac, then varnish, and antiquing with wax and rottenstone: about three days.

    Total: twelve days maximum.

Additional materials

Gesso, glaze, flat varnish, shellac (optional), rottenstone, and wax.

Preparing the surface

Remove any existing drawer knobs, fill the holes with plastic wood, and sand off any excess. If the chest has been finished with paint or varnish that is at all slick, sand it until the surface has a tooth. Remove all traces of old wax. Give the entire surface a coat of gesso. When it is dry, add a second coat. While the second coat is still wet, add signs of age and distress. When both coats of the gesso are completely dry, apply an antique glaze over the gesso. Do not begin stenciling until the following day.

Preparing the stencils

Mark all stencils carefully, identifying the top as well as the colors. Draw the register marks on the

Green

Cinnamon

Project 6

Early American chest of drawers

(Plate 36, page 78)
14 stencils, 5 colors

A chest of drawers, adapted from an early eighteenth-century piece, faithfully reproduces the colors of the original. The chest was heavily antiqued to imitate the aged condition of its predecessor. Brass drawer pulls, specially purchased, were darkened with a tinted flat varnish. For a more contemporary look, the heavy antiquing might be omitted.

stencils for the circular polychrome design very accurately because all the shapes must fit together precisely. Divide the black vertical border shapes onto two stencils to avoid breakage (see page 29). The black and beige parts of the small center design on the drawers may go on one stencil. Designs for the vertical border, the center of the drawer, and the base are on pages 138–140.

Measuring and marking off
Only the running border around the base of the chest need be measured and marked. Start stenciling this border from the center of the base so that the design will come out evenly at both ends. Adapt the placing of the design to the dimensions of the chest.

Stenciling
Begin with the periwinkle blue stripe bordering the drawers. For the blue, mix:

> 1 tablespoon white japan paint
> ¼ teaspoon ultramarine blue japan paint
> ¼ teaspoon dioxide purple (artists' oil) paint

1. Print the blue stripe on one corner of a drawer and do the same on the corners of all the drawers, turning and reversing the stencil to fit the corners as necessary.
2. Stencil all the black on the vertical borders of the chest before going ahead with the other colors. Begin with the two stencils for the little vertical design that runs up each of the sides of the chest, printing both on the front and sides of the chest.
3. Print the black stencil for the polychrome design inside the periwinkle blue border. Stencil the *left* side of the drawer and replace the same stencil on the *right* side of the drawer in an upside-down position. Invert the stencil each time it is printed so you have a more varied design. (When you print the rest of the stencils for this design, they too should be inverted alternately.)

Print blue stripe on drawers.

Add black vertical borders.

Continue with black on base and drawers.

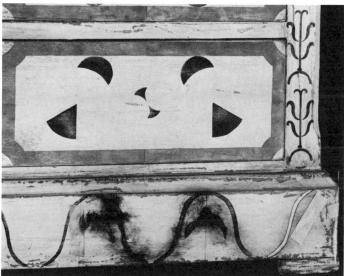

Beige Red
Black Brown
Blue

Vertical border design.

Reversing stencil (page 140, top) for opposite end of base.

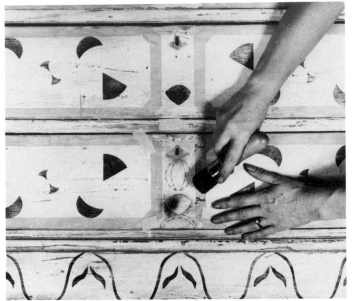

Printing black and beige in center design.

4. Stencil the black part of the border at the base of the chest. Begin at the middle of the base so the design will come out evenly on both ends. Block out any surplus shapes. Add the little extra incurving piece on each end of the border.

5. Place the center design precisely under the keyhole. The *black* stencil has the cutout for the *beige* shape on it, so print both black and beige while the stencil is taped in position. For the beige, mix:

    2 teaspoons white japan paint
    1 teaspoon raw sienna japan paint

Print the black and beige stencil in the center of each of the drawers.

6. Finish this center design with the red and brown stencils. Mix the *red* as follows:

    1 teaspoon chrome yellow orange japan paint
    1/2 teaspoon American vermilion japan paint

Mix the *brown* as follows:

    1 teaspoon white japan paint
    1 teaspoon raw sienna japan paint
    1 teaspoon burnt sienna japan paint

Complete the design on all the drawers.

7. Returning to the polychrome design, complete the beige, red, and brown stencils on all the drawers, being sure to invert each stencil alternately as you did with the black stencil. Use the register marks for correct placement.

8. Complete the front and sides of the base with the beige and brown parts of the design.

Adding red, brown, and beige to polychrome design.

Filling in beige and brown on base.

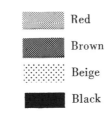

Let the stenciling dry at least three days befor applying any finish.

	Red
	Brown
	Beige
	Black

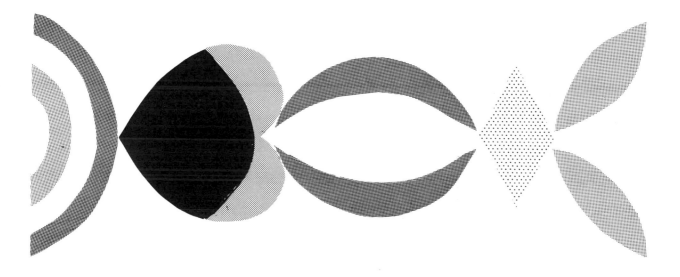

Design for end of base.

Finishing

Before you varnish over the stenciling, test the colors to be sure they will not run. If necessary, isolate the stenciling with a protective coat of shellac. Varnish the entire chest with one coat of flat varnish. Final touches of antiquity may be added by applying rottenstone and wax. Drill appropriate holes for the new drawer pulls. If the brass is too bright, coat it with a small amount of raw umber japan paint mixed with satin varnish before putting the drawer pulls on the chest.

Base design.   ▨ Beige   ■ Black   ▨ Brown

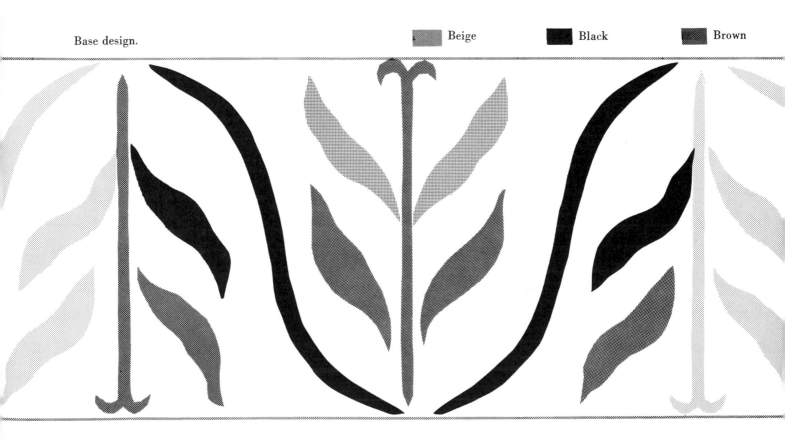

Project 7

Moroccan door and rug

(Plate 16, page 73)

Door: 11 stencils, 4 colors; rug: 5 stencils, 2 colors
Project 7 is presented in two parts. The designs on the door panels are copied from a paneled Moroccan door, using the original color scheme. Islamic designs on the heavy cotton canvas rug have been stenciled in two shades of blue against a white background. Several coats of varnish protect the stenciling. The finished rug combines the dual advantages of a rug and a painted floor; it is both ornamental and practical.

The door

Time

1. Preparation, including sanding down the panels (one hour) and applying two consecutive coats of varnish: one day.
2. Applying glaze and cutting stencils: one or two days. Stencils are cut while the glaze dries.
3. Painting the blue surround: one hour, plus one hour to dry.
4. Striping the panels: about one day.
5. Stenciling the design: one to two days, plus three days to dry.
6. Varnishing: about half an hour, plus a day to dry.
7. Antiquing with rottenstone and wax: one hour.
   Total: twelve days maximum.

Additional materials

One contemporary stock paneled door. The one illustrated measures $31\frac{1}{2}'' \times 77\frac{1}{2}''$, but the designs might be adapted for panels of different dimensions. On a flush door, an illusion of paneling can be created by making rectangles of an appropriate size with the same striping used to outline the carved panels. Also: one flat $\frac{3}{4}''$ sable brush, one standard $3''$ paintbrush, rottenstone and wax, gesso, glaze, flat or satin varnish, and sandpaper or an electric sander.

Preparing the surface

Paneled doors have a slightly raised section within each panel which must be sanded level. Speed up the job with an electric sander and finish sanding by hand. Sand the whole door if it is secondhand or prefinished. Apply two coats of gesso. When it is completely dry, add a coat of glaze, mixing:

> $\frac{1}{2}$ cup flat varnish
> $\frac{1}{4}$ teaspoon Prussian blue japan paint

The varnish should be very delicately tinted with the blue to make it just off-white. Cover the entire side of the door and allow it to dry completely before you begin decorating.

Preparing the stencils

Trace the design for the top panels onto the acetate. The green should be divided onto two stencils to eliminate gaps in the printing. Number them "Green 1" and "Green 2."

The design for the four large panels is presented in two parts because of the book's space limitations, but the stencils for the entire design should be

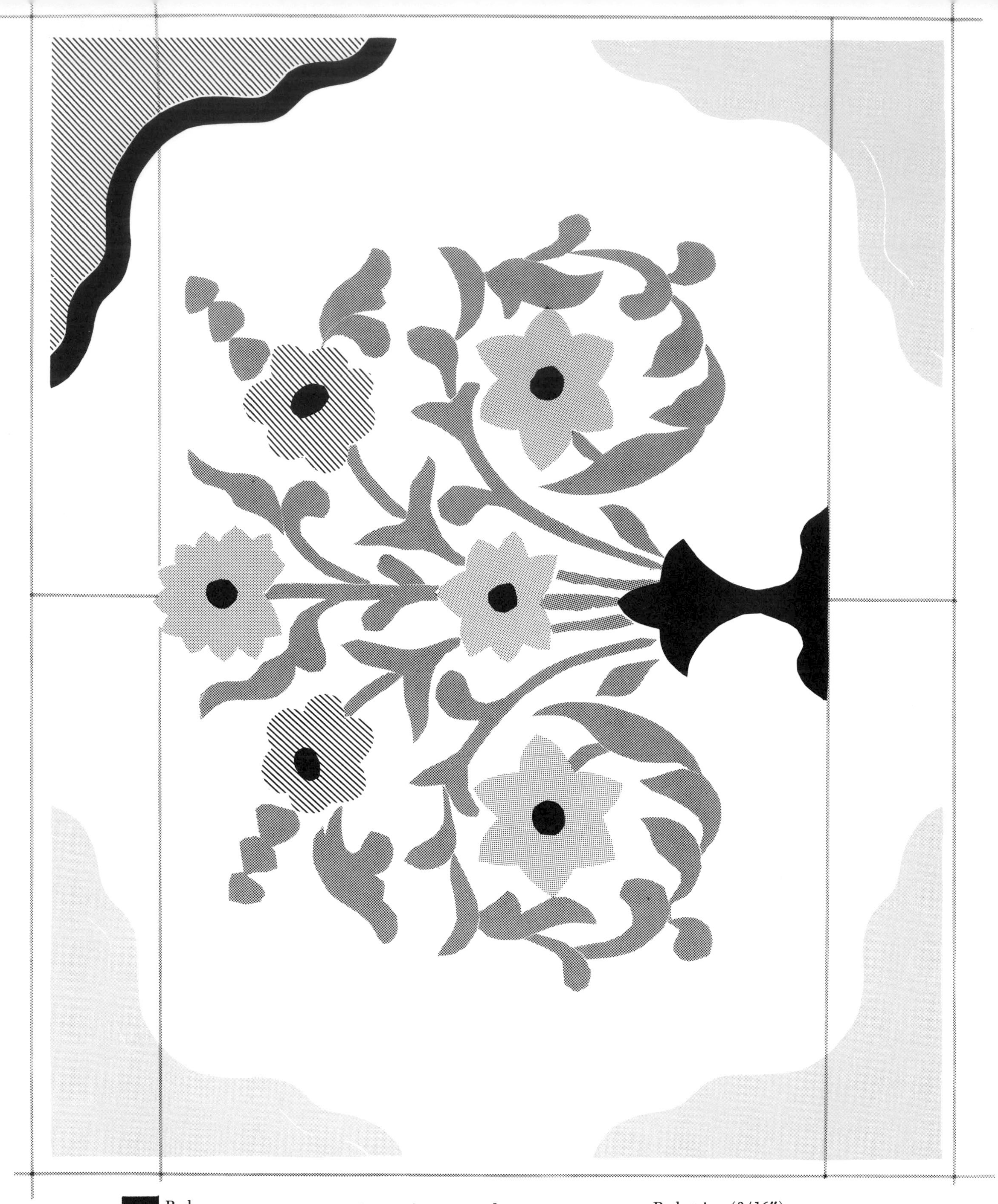

Design for top panel.

Red

Blue

Yellow

Green

Red stripe (3/16″)

Yellow stripe inside molding (3/16″)

Yellow stripe on curved molding (3/8″)

White stripe outside panel (5/16″)

traced on single sheets of acetate. Because the red shapes are so close together and the green is continuous, the red and the green should be divided onto two stencils and marked and numbered. The little corner design, which comes in two parts (blue and red), is stenciled in each corner of all the panels. Because of its shape, the corner stencil is vulnerable to tearing; reinforce the outer edge with Scotch tape. On the yellow stencil for the large panels, outline the feet of the urn with prominent register marks in black ink—they will be your guide for placing the stencil in the panel. The blue part of the urn may be cut on the same stencil as Green 2. The design for the long panels is on pages 146–147.

Measuring and marking
Measure and mark a vertical line down the center of each panel as a guide for positioning the designs.

To mark the stripes, follow the diagram, drawing the lines lightly with a pencil. Make one line each for the white stripe, the yellow stripe, and the red stripe. The measurements are shown in the diagram.

Striping
Mask off the white stripe around the outside of the panels with tape and paint the surrounding area blue. Paint up to the masking tape, being careful not to let the paint seep under it. (When the tape is removed, you should have a clean white stripe left around each of the panels.) To mix the blue, use:

> 3 tablespoons of white japan paint
> 3 tablespoons of ultramarine blue japan
>   paint
> ½ teaspoon of raw umber japan paint

Use a good quality 3″ brush to paint the blue area. Save any leftover blue paint for stenciling. Float a small amount of turpentine over the paint in the saucer and cover it with plastic wrap to keep it from drying up.

When the blue paint is dry to the touch (in about one hour), remove the masking tape. Clean any run-under off the white stripe. Apply fresh strips of tape over the white stripe. Put more strips of tape

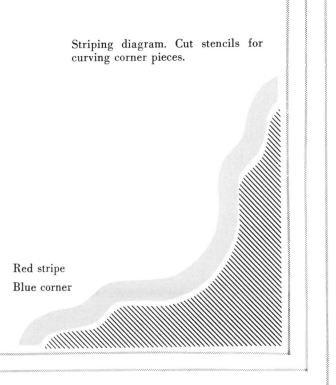

Striping diagram. Cut stencils for curving corner pieces.

Red stripe
Blue corner

Flexible flat paint brush fills in yellow stripe on curved molding.

Acetate gives straight red stripe a clean edge. Tape masks yellow.

around on the *inside* of the panel to form the inner edge of the yellow stripe. With the little flat sable brush, paint in the yellow stripe. Mix the yellow, using:

> 2 teaspoons medium yellow japan paint
> 1/4 teaspoon raw sienna japan paint

Do not load the brush with too much paint. Save at least one teaspoon of paint for additional stenciling the following day. Remove all the tape. When the yellow stripe is dry to the touch, apply fresh strips of masking tape over it, along the inside edge, as a guide for the red stripe.

Use a stencil brush for the red stripe. Mix the red paint using:

> 2 teaspoons American vermilion light
> japan paint
> 1 teaspoon Venetian red japan paint

Use a straight piece of acetate as a guide to give the red stripe a clean, sharp inner edge. Save leftover red paint for stenciling. Leave the masking tape in place. You will be stenciling the little corners next, and the tape protects the yellow stripe from becoming smudged as you stencil in the curved red stripe across the corners.

Stenciling
1. Print the little red corner stencil in each corner of all the panels.
2. Stencil the blue in all the corners, using the paint saved earlier. Remove all strips of masking tape.

3. Stencil the center design in the two top panels. Place the yellow stencil in the center, lining it up with the penciled guidelines made on the panel. Add the blue and the red stencils for this center design.
4. Finish with the stencils for the foliage, Green 1 and Green 2, using:

> 1 teaspoon chrome green light japan paint

Now stencil the four large panels. (One pair of the panels is longer than the other. This does not affect the design; there will just be more white space above it.)
1. Start by centering the yellow stencil on the pencil line. Be sure the register marks showing the feet of the urn are centered between the bottom corners. The feet will be printed by the next stencil, Red 1.
2. Print Red 2, then Green 1.
3. Green 2 and the blue part of the urn, cut on the same stencil, are done next. Complete the design on all four panels.

Finishing
Allow stenciling to dry for a minimum of three days. Before varnishing, test the red paint. If it shows a tendency to dissolve, spray some shellac over the stenciling. When the shellac is dry, coat the entire door with flat or satin-finish varnish. If possible, lay the door flat while varnishing, to discourage runs. The door may be lightly antiqued with rottenstone and wax the following day. Polish well after the wax has dried.

Curved red stripe is painted next.

Yellow stencil is centered in panel. Red is added.

Blue and green are added.

Pencil line centers yellow stencil.

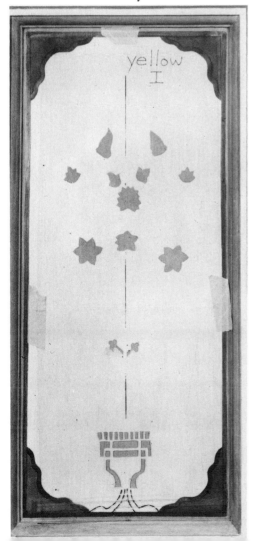

Red I and II follow the yellow.

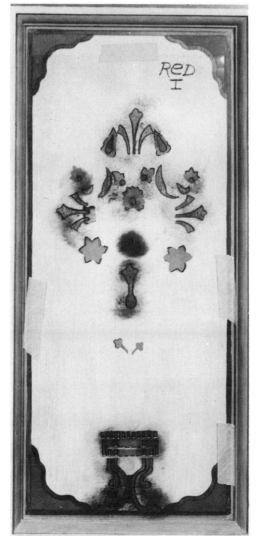

Green and blue complete the design.

Design for long panels. In tracing, overlap the two sections to
make single long stencils of the
full design. Distribute vulnerable
red and green shapes on two stencils each.

146

Red

Yellow

Blue

Green

147

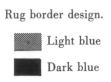

The rug

Time

1. Sizing both sides of the canvas: two hours.
2. Preparing the stencils: two hours.
3. Measuring and marking the surface: one hour.
4. Stenciling: from two to three days.
5. Varnishing may be done four days after the stenciling. Three coats are needed.
6. Putting a backing on the rug: about one hour.

Additional materials

A 42″ × 72″ piece of very heavy cotton duck canvas; a 36″ metal ruler, gesso, Elmer's Glue-All, one 3″ nylon brush, one 3″ varnish brush, flat or satin-finish varnish, several large sheets of heavy brown wrapping paper, two yards of white or tan burlap 45″ wide, and (optionally) two and one-half yards of off-white woven fringe.

Preparing the surface

Spread several sheets of heavy brown wrapping paper on a well-swept floor. Roll the canvas out on the paper. Although the canvas is 42″ × 72″, the design is only 42″ × 69″. The extra inches allow for turning under the cut edges and for any shrinkage that occurs when the rug is sized. Using long strips of masking tape, mask off 1″ along the cut edges of the canvas.

Sizing

In a clean bowl or coffee can, mix:

> ½ cup of gesso
> ½ cup of Elmer's Glue-All
> ½ cup of water

Stir this sizing mixture well with a spoon and apply it with a 3″ brush first to one side of the rug and then, when this first coat is dry, to the other side. Coat the rug well. Remove the strips of masking tape from both sides of the rug. Wait until the following day to start stenciling. Sizing both sides of the rug helps make it lie flat so it will not need to be tacked down while it is stenciled.

Preparing the stencils

Trace the border design, dividing the dark blue

onto two stencils as illustrated on page 151. Mark the horizontal lines on your stencils carefully as they represent the areas where the striping will go. Leave at least a 1½″ margin around the entire design. Mark the "Top" and the color identification on each of the stencils: Stencil 1 dark blue and Stencil 2 dark blue.

Trace the center design to be stenciled in the center of the rug. The design measures 9″ × 9″. Only half of it is illustrated here; trace it double. Allow a generous margin of acetate around the design on each stencil. The design (page 153) must be divided onto three stencils: Stencil 1 dark blue, Stencil 2 dark blue, and Stencil 3 light blue.

The cutouts in the stencils must be precise. After tracing, go over all the outlines on the stencils with your technical drawing pen and a metal ruler. The shapes are easy to cut out, but the cutting must be done exactly on the line so that when the stencil is printed the parts will fit together perfectly.

Measuring and marking

Using a metal ruler, measure off a border area approximately 7½″ wide all around the rug. The center area must measure exactly 27″ by 54″. Any discrepancy in the size of the canvas due to shrinking should be made up in the border rather than in the center section of the rug. Adjust the width of the border to give the center area its full dimensions. Next, measure and mark off the inside area into eighteen precise 9″ squares. Mark lightly in pencil.

Stenciling

Begin with the dark blue border design. Mix:

> 2 tablespoons ultramarine blue japan paint
> 2 tablespoons white japan paint
> ¼ teaspoon raw umber japan paint

Thin the mixture slightly with turpentine. Canvas soaks up paint more readily than other surfaces, so add turpentine occasionally to keep the paint moist and the brush from caking. Store the paint mixture in a small jar, using small quantities as needed.

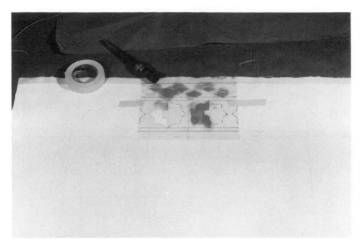 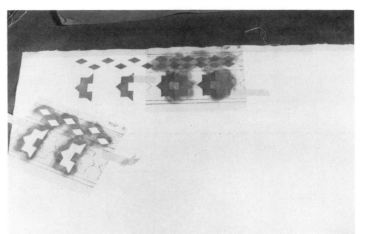

1. Begin with border Stencil 1 at one end of the rug. Make a small pencil mark at the exact center of the border. Place the stencil so this center mark lies between the two star shapes and print the stencil.

2. Place the second border stencil in position and print it, also in dark blue.

 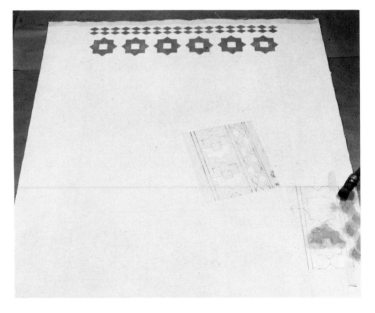

3. Reprint both these stencils until you have six completed stars and the little diamond border on one end of the rug. Do the same on the opposite end.

4. Print the same design on the long side of the rug; make a pencil mark at the exact center of the border. Place the *middle* of one of the stars on this center mark and print the stencil.

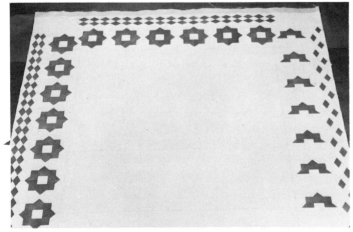 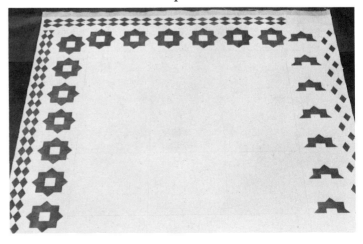

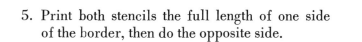

5. Print both stencils the full length of one side of the border, then do the opposite side.

6. As you print the rows of diamond shapes around the outer edge, block out portions of the diamonds with masking tape at the corners, thus leaving room for the striping.

Divide the dark blue shapes of the border design onto two separate stencils.

7. As you print the center of the rug, protect the border with a piece of heavy wrapping paper. The center section may be stenciled by doing all the dark blue first, or by printing one square at a time in both shades. Place the stencil for Dark Blue 1 in one of the squares first and follow with Dark Blue 2.

8. Place the third stencil in correct position and print the lighter blue, using:

    1 teaspoon cerulean blue artists' oil paint
    4 teaspoons white japan paint
    1 teaspoon Prussian blue japan paint

9. To make the stripes, use two strips of acetate as guides. Except for the outside one, which is slightly narrower, all the stripes are ½″ wide. There is no need to measure and mark off the rug for the stripes because they fit precisely between units of the design. When doing the outside stripe, adjust the width to whatever space remains—anywhere from ¼″ to ½″.

10. Butt the striping at the ends of the rug against the side stripes.

11. When the striping is finished, check the entire surface for unintentional gaps between the design units and make any necessary corrections. Allow a minimum of three days before varnishing.

Light blue
Dark blue

Design for center of rug. Divide dark blue onto two stencils.

Finishing

The rug should have at least three coats of varnish. Giving it four coats is better. Use a flat or satin finish and allow a day's drying time between each of the coats. Satin-finish varnish is more durable. The varnish may be very slightly tinted with a bit of cerulean blue artists' oil paint, thoroughly mixed. Varnish over the stenciled surface with a good-quality varnish brush. Do not varnish the two end strips that are to be turned under when the varnishing has been completed.

When the varnish is fully dry, turn the rug upside down on brown paper and fold the end strips to the back, making a good crease. Using a small brush or applicator, apply glue under the edge and press these hems down very flat. Apply something heavy to keep them flat while the glue is drying. If a fringe is to be applied, cut two pieces of fringe to the exact width of the rug and, while it is still upside down, glue the woven edge of the fringe in place.

When the glue is dry, apply the burlap backing to the underside of the rug. The burlap must be smooth; iron out any wrinkles. Place the burlap over the reverse side of the rug. Turn the edges of the burlap under on all four sides with a sharp crease, making a 1½" hem on all four sides. Apply glue to the edges of the canvas and press and weigh the burlap down on it.

The finished rug may be cleaned by wiping it with a sponge or cloth and warm water and mild soap. The rug may be rolled up loosely for moving or temporary storage. Nailing or tacking the rug to the floor is unnecessary and inadvisable. A thin rubber cushion will prevent slipping and help to protect the rug against wear.

Project 8

Geometric floor design

(Plate 37, page 79)
3 stencils, 3 colors

Inspired by an old American quilt, this geometric design was stenciled on a painted white background in colors suitable for a contemporary room. It is the only one of the eight projects that can successfully be done entirely with a roller. The directions here suggest using acetate stencils, but paper stencils could be used instead. The design shapes are arranged on the stencils in such a way that, although square stencils are used on a squared-off surface, a diagonal pattern is achieved. The color combination could, of course, be changed to suit any decorating scheme. The amounts of paint listed and the time estimated are for stenciling a floor not much larger than 15′ × 15′.

Time
1. Preparation of floor (following sanding): three days, including a first coat of paint, light hand-sanding, and second coat, and one day to dry (more than one day in damp weather).
2. Marking: half a day.
3. Preparation of stencils: an hour or two, while the paint is drying.
4. Stenciling: at average speed, one day for each of the three colors.
5. Drying: three days.
6. Finishing: a few hours on two successive days, plus at least one day to dry.
   Total: twelve and a half days minimum.

Additional materials
Extra-large acetate and tracing paper, one gallon white oil-base floor paint, one gallon turpentine, artists' oil color, three 7″ mohair rollers for stenciling, two broad brushes for preparation and finishing, one gallon varnish.

Preparation of the floor
Have the floor sanded, and clean up all dust with a vacuum cleaner and a tack cloth. Brush on the plain white oil-base paint. (As a timesaver, water-base paint may be substituted and applied with a roller.)

Preparation of stencils
In addition to the usual equipment, you will need a sheet of tracing paper at least 18″ × 18″ and a T square. For the stencils, you will need two sheets of acetate 24″ × 24″ and one sheet 12″ × 12″. The design given on page 159 is one-quarter of the whole design. All the shapes are cut just *outside* the traced lines.

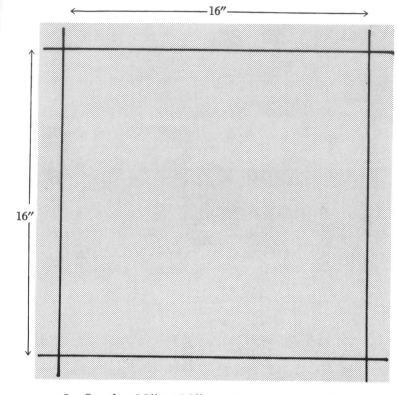

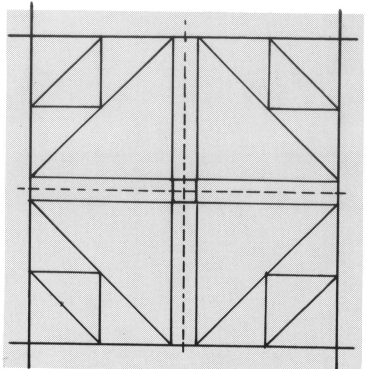

1. On the 18″ × 18″ tracing paper, and with a T square as a guide, draw four lines forming a perfect 16″ × 16″ square. In this project these solid lines are your *registration* lines, and they must be put on *all* the stencils.

2. Divide the 16″ square into four equal parts as shown by the broken line and trace the design on page 159 into each one of them, turning it in four directions to make one complete repeat of the design, as shown in the diagram above.

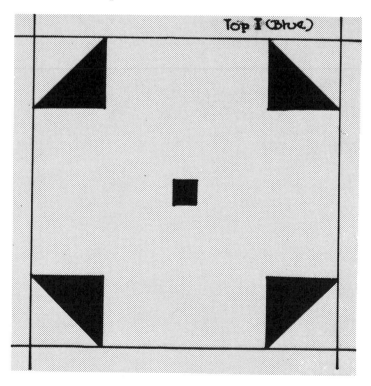

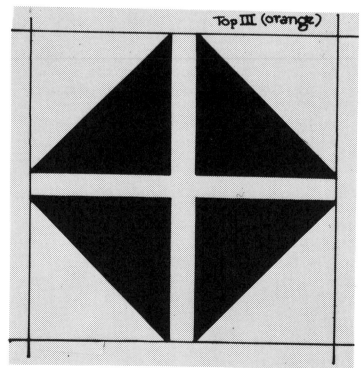

3. Tape the tracing paper to a flat surface. Center the first 24″ × 24″ sheet of acetate over the tracing and tape it down. Trace the small center square, the small triangles, and the registration lines that surround the large square. Mark the upper edge of the stencil "Top I."

4. Leaving this stencil in place, tape the second 24″ × 24″ acetate sheet exactly over it. Trace the registration lines and the large triangles. Mark the upper edge of the stencil "Top III." This stencil is for printing the orange.

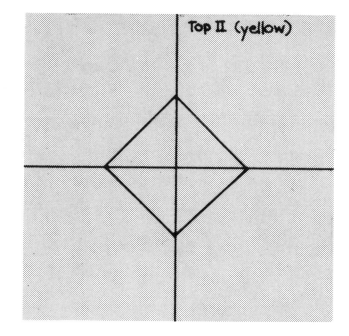

Top II (yellow)

5. For the yellow stencil, a different process is followed. Take the 12″ × 12″ sheet of acetate and mark a large plus mark in the exact center, extending it all the way out to the edges so that it forms an upright cross which precisely bisects the stencil in both directions. Mark the upper edge "Top II." Place the center of the plus mark over the point where the registration lines meet in one corner of the design. Trace the corner triangle onto the acetate. Move the acetate from corner to corner, keeping the "Top" up at all times, and trace each of the corner triangles onto the acetate until you have formed the diamond. Cut the diamond shape out of the acetate. When the stencil is printed, the lines extending out to the margins will line up with the intersections of the grid drawn on the floor, registering the yellow diamond in the space formed by the printing of the blue triangles.

Marking and measuring
Start at the center, lightly mark the floor in a grid of 16″ squares. If the outer squares of the grid are not a full 16″, leave a border of several inches so that you can gracefully terminate the all-over pattern by blocking out parts of the design.

Mixing the paint
You will need large amounts of stencil paint to cover the floor, plus one gallon of turpentine to thin it sufficiently for application with a roller.

Mix each color in a large glass bowl or other suitable container, thinning it with the turpentine to the proper consistency. Pour the mixture into a can and cap it tightly until you are ready to begin stenciling. Clean the bowl thoroughly before mixing the next color. As you begin each mixture, hold back a little of the basic color so that you can moderate the hue if you find you have misjudged and added too much of the other colors. For the blue, you will need:

½ pint flake white japan paint
1 ounce ultramarine blue japan paint
2 tubes cobalt violet artists' oil color,
    preferably Winsor & Newton

Pour most of the can of white into the bowl. Thin slightly with turpentine and start to add very small amounts of the ultramarine blue. A little goes a long way, and you will need only between five and seven teaspoons of blue in this amount of white. Add a tube of the cobalt violet, working it out together first with some of the japan paint with a palette knife on a sheet of glass or a saucer. You may need the second tube of cobalt violet to get the periwinkle blue shown in the color plate. (The cobalt violet used for this floor was Winsor & Newton's. Other brands will produce a slightly different shade of blue.) Gradually add it to the first mixture until you get the right color, and test it on a white surface before you put it in a can and cap it.

For the yellow, thin with turpentine to rolling consistency:

½ pint chrome yellow LL japan paint

Put one-third of the yellow aside, to be mixed with:

½ pint American vermilion L

to make the orange.

Pour most of the vermilion into the bowl. Thin slightly with turpentine. Add the yellow cautiously, testing a greatly thinned sample from time to time, stroking it onto a white surface with a brush. It takes about three parts vermilion to one of yellow to get the orange shown in the color plate, but mix it so that it looks right to you in combination with the colors already mixed, rather than trying to reproduce exactly what may be discerned in the photograph.

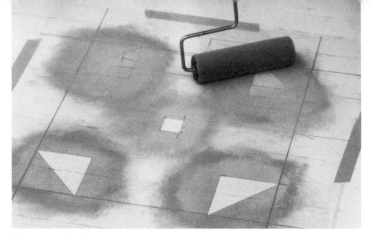

Blue stencil lines up with squares marked on floor.

As the blue is printed across the floor, the triangles meet to form squares.

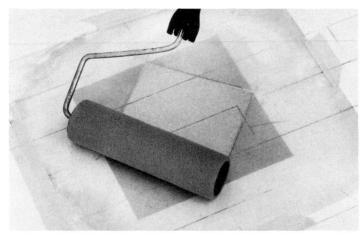

The yellow is printed within the squares formed by the blue triangles.

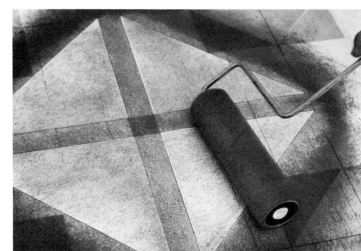

Orange stencil, lined up with squares on floor, completes the pattern.

Stenciling

Arrange your equipment in such a way that it is convenient to move about, with separate mohair rollers for each color. As you will have noted while tracing the design, the blue and orange stencils are placed within the squares formed by the grid and the yellow stencils are placed at the intersections of the squares.

1. Start with Stencil 1 and the blue paint. The mixture should have a consistency more like milk than cream; try a print where it will not be conspicuous and thin or thicken the paint as needed. Remember to keep the *top* side of the stencil turned consistently in only one direction. Place the stencil in the first square and print it.
2. Print the blue all across the floor.
3. The yellow (Stencil 2) is printed next because it must fit within the space formed by the bases of the blue triangles.
4. Now print all the orange, placing the stencils within the squares marked on the floor. This is by far the greatest part of the stenciling in this project and may take a day or more to do, even with two people working.

Clean up any smeared or tracked paint with a turpentine-dampened tissue, masking off adjacent stenciling with tape, and touch up wherever necessary with the background paint and a small brush. Allow at least three days' drying time, then remove the chalk lines with a kneaded eraser before varnishing.

Finishing

Protect the stenciling with two coats of varnish.

This design shows only one quarter of the stencil. Rotate tracing paper as described on page 156 to make the full stencil pattern. For the yellow stencil, follow directions on page 157.

■ Blue

▨ Orange

▦ Yellow

11. Design

An important aspect of stenciling is knowing how to choose the right design for a particular purpose and how to adapt it to your specific needs. As you become more and more familiar with the types of design most adaptable to stenciling, you will be more readily able to calculate exactly how many stencils will be needed and how they can be most effectively handled. This will be an asset in helping you to choose a design that is both practical and beautiful.

The designs reproduced in this book have already been adapted for stenciling. Each gray tone represents a different color in the design. Sometimes you will have to distribute parts of a single color onto more than one stencil, either to eliminate gaps between them when they are printed or to make a sufficiently strong stencil. However, remember that sometimes more than one color may be printed from a single stencil if the design shapes are far enough apart.

The flat tones of gray in which the designs are presented make clear the division of colors but do not show the delicate shading that can be attained with good brush technique. It is the stenciler's own skill, taste, and imagination in handling shading that give the designs the depth and individuality apparent in the examples shown in color.

Sources of design

You do not have to be an artist to create your own designs. Inspiration and opportunity lie all around you, not only in books and magazines but in printed fabrics, wallpaper, china, embroidery, photographs, lace, decorated ribbon, woven geometric patterns, grillwork, rugs, inlaid wood, hand-painted furniture, and tinware, tiles, and other decorated objects and surfaces. Design is a process of bringing together interesting forms and colors in ways that are pleasing and effective, and the elements from which new designs may be developed could be found anywhere.

Museums are great sources of inspiration and often sell slides, postcards, prints, or catalogues covering many of their collections. Pages from library books that are not available for borrowing may often be photocopied on the library's own machines. Many good design books are now sold in paperback editions. Establishing your own collection of designs from such sources can be very rewarding. If you are looking for designs you intend to reproduce for sale, you must, of course, confine copying to works that are in the public domain; you must not borrow designs that are under copyright or are the property of others. However, there is a rich store of historical material from many cultures to be drawn upon, and the more you study them all, the less dependent you will be upon the ideas of others, and the more readily you will begin to create new designs of your own. Keep alert. Some of the best designs we have worked with have been stumbled upon quite by accident when we were not especially looking for them. Train your eye and your mind to be receptive to beautiful design wherever you are!

Some designs, because of their nature, can be used in more than one way. An entire piece may be stenciled with a single design used in a number of different ways. A single design can become quite versatile if you change one or more of the colors, reverse the stencil, print the design end-to-end, or use it as an all-over pattern. The following examples illustrate this.

A single design repeated horizontally to form a border. ▲

The same design reversed and placed base-to-base with the original takes on an entirely different character. ▶

Rearrangement in a group of four radiating outward from the center makes the design seem entirely new and different. ▼

A simple floral design.

The same design reversed.

Reversing the stencil so the design faces left and right along a horizontal line.

Printing the design end-to-end, alternately reversing the stencil.

The design alternated with a simple daisy motif to form an all-over pattern.

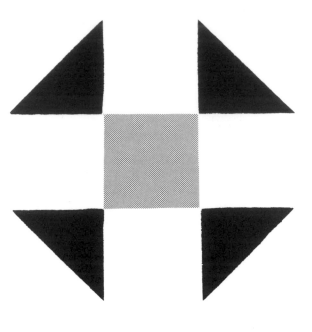

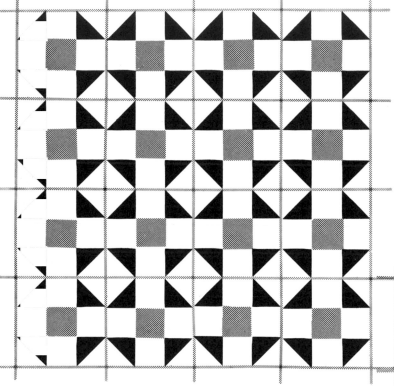

To make an all-over pattern with a design like this one . . .

. . . the surface is squared off in a grid and the design is placed within each square.

To produce a checkerboard effect, the design is printed in every other square.

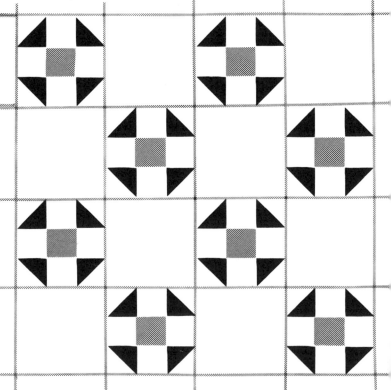

A flowing design form like this sprig is more easily arranged by placing it at the intersections of the grid. The spacing is the same, but registration by placing the plus mark drawn on the stencil over the intersections is more exact. ▲

Reversing the stencil for every other print in the half-drop repeat achieves still more grace and variety. ▼

Placing the sprig at every other intersection produces the variation of a "half-drop repeat."

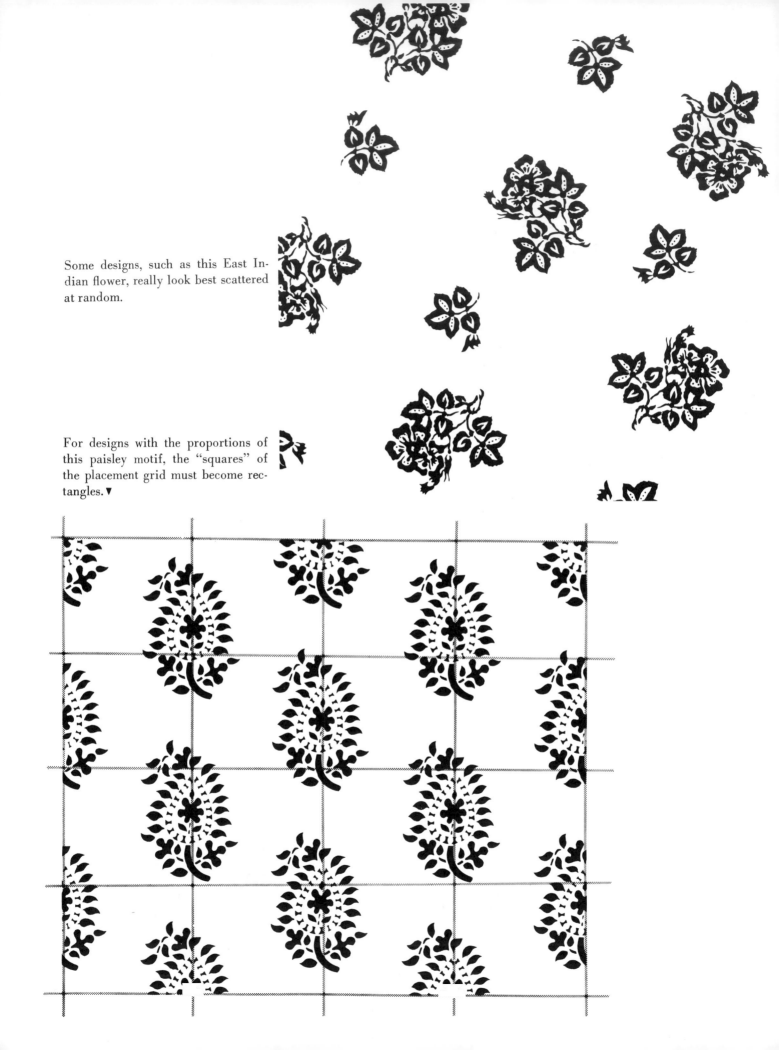

Some designs, such as this East Indian flower, really look best scattered at random.

For designs with the proportions of this paisley motif, the "squares" of the placement grid must become rectangles. ▼

Copying a design

The simplest way to copy a design is to lay tracing paper over it and trace its outlines. You may find that some of the shapes in designs derived from paintings, photographs, or other sources must be altered to render them more practical for stenciling. It is better to make these corrections on the tracing paper rather than afterward on the stencil. When you are satisfied with your improved version, trace it onto the stencil material.

When it is not possible to trace a design, you have to draw it freehand. This calls for a certain amount of technical skill and a well-trained eye for detail. It is often some quite subtle yet important quality or characteristic that makes a design appealing. When you look at a chosen design, try to analyze and interpret these qualities in the version you prepare for stenciling.

Altering the size of a design

You can reduce or enlarge a design either by having it photostated in a new size or by mechanically squaring it off on paper. Photostating, although not cheap in itself, saves hours of valuable time. It also assures accuracy. The negative or first stage in the photostating process is as easy to trace from as the positive, and is less expensive. Designs may be photostated directly from a book or magazine.

For photostating, mark the new width at the top of the original, indicating the outer limits of the design with arrows, as shown. This is sufficient for most purposes. If the design is to fit a specific space, however, the exact dimensions of the rescaled design may be determined by another procedure.

Start with a piece of tracing paper large enough to accommodate the new size of the design. Place the tracing paper over the original and draw a rectangle around the part of the design you intend to use. Draw a diagonal from one corner of the rectangle to the opposite one (and beyond it if the design is to be enlarged) as shown in the diagram. Select any point on the diagonal that represents the chosen width (or height) of the design. Draw a new vertical and a new horizontal line from that point, parallel to those already drawn, forming a new rectangle. This will show you what the full proportions of the enlarged or reduced design will be.

To alter the size of the design by squaring it off, trace it onto a piece of tracing paper. Draw a rectangle around the design. Divide the rectangle into equal squares. Number each square. On another sheet of paper draw a rectangle in the size you want the design to be, and divide this into the same number of squares as the first rectangle. Number these squares too. Next, copy exactly onto each square the details found in the original.

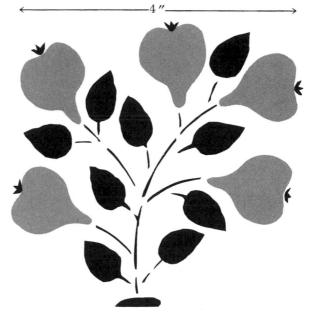

Marking a design for photostating.

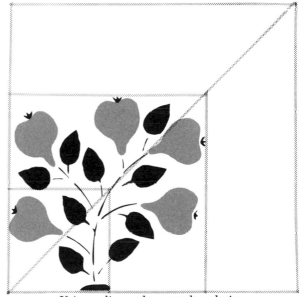

Using a diagonal to rescale a design.

Squaring off a design to alter the size.

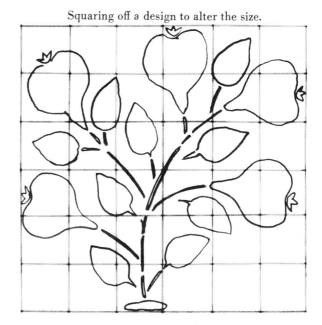

12. Design Gallery

E PLURIBUS UNUM

Bibliography

Audsley, W. and G. *Designs and Patterns from Historic Ornament*. New York: Dover Publications, Inc., 1968.

Berendsen, Anne, *et al. Tiles: A General History*. New York: The Viking Press, Inc., 1967.

Balfour, Henry. "The Origin of Stencilling in the Fiji Islands." Reprinted from the *Journal of the Royal Anthropological Institute of Great Britain and Ireland*, Vol. 54, pp. 347–352. London, 1924.

Birrell, Verla. *The Textile Arts*. New York: Harper and Row, 1959.

Calvert, James. *Fiji, Then and Now*. New York: D. Appleton & Co., 1859.

Christie, Archibald H. *Pattern Design*. New York: Dover Publications, Inc., 1969.

Cramer, Edith. *Handbook of Early American Decoration*. Boston: Charles T. Branford Company, 1951.

Edwards, Edward B. *Pattern and Design with Dynamic Symmetry*. New York: Dover Publications, Inc., 1967.

Enciso, George. *Design Motifs of Ancient Mexico*. New York: Dover Publications, Inc., 1953.

Fales, Dean A., Jr. *American Painted Furniture 1660–1880*, Bishop, Robert C., ed. New York: E. P. Dutton & Co., Inc., 1972.

Gillon, Edmund V., Jr. *Victorian Designs for Design and Decoration*. New York: Dover Publications, Inc., 1968.

Glass, Frederick James. *Stencil Craft*. London: University of London Press, 1927.

Hansen. H. J. *European Folk Art*. New York: McGraw-Hill, Inc., 1968.

Hart, E. *Stencils of Old Japan: From the Collection of E. Hart, with Introductory Note*. London, 1825.

Hornung, Clarence P. *Treasury of American Design*, Vols. 1 and 2. New York: Harry N. Abrams, Inc., 1972.

Koch, Robert. *Louis C. Tiffany, Rebel in Glass*. New York: Crown Publishers and Robert Koch, 1964.

Korf, Dingeman. *Dutch Tiles*. New York: Universe Books, 1964.

Lipman, Jean. *American Folk Decoration, with Practical Instruction by Eve Meulendyke*. New York: Dover Publications, Inc., 1972.

Lipman, Jean, and Winchester, Alice. *The Flowering of American Folk Art: 1776–1876*. New York: The Viking Press, Inc., 1974. London: Thames and Hudson, 1974.

Little, Nina Fletcher. *American Decorative Wall Painting*. Sturbridge, Massachusetts: Old Sturbridge Village in cooperation with The Studio Publications, Inc., New York and London, 1952.

McConnell, Jane, and McConnell, Burt. *The White House*. New York and London: The Studio Publications, Inc., 1954.

Meier, Henry. "Woodcut Stencils of Four Hundred Years Ago," *New York Public Library Bulletin*, Vol. 42, pp. 10–19. New York, 1938.

Meyer, Franz Sales. *Handbook of Ornament*. New York: Dover Publications, Inc., 1957.

O'Neil, Isabel. *The Art of the Painted Finish*. New York: William Morrow & Co., Inc., 1971.

Plath, Iona. *Decorative Arts of Sweden*. New York: Dover Publications, Inc., 1965.

Reader, Francis. *Stencilled Wall-Paintings, Northleach, Gloucestershire*. Bristol, England: Bristol and Gloucestershire Archaeological Society, 1939.

Rice, Stanley. *Getting Started in Prints and Patterns*. New York: Bruce Publishing Co., 1971.

Ritz, Gislind M. *The Art of Painted Furniture*. New York: Van Nostrand Reinhold Company, 1972.

Sabine, Ellen. *Early American Decorative Patterns and How to Paint Them*. Princeton, New Jersey: D. Reinhold Company, Inc., 1962.

———. *American Antique Decoration*. Princeton, New Jersey: D. Reinhold Company, Inc., 1956.

Smith, Corinna Lindon. *Interesting People: Eighty Years with the Great and Near Great*. Norman, Oklahoma: University of Oklahoma Press, 1962.

Speltz, Alexander. *The Styles of Ornament*. New York: Dover Publications, Inc., 1959.

Stein, Sir Mark Aurel. *Serindia*, Vols. 1–3. Oxford, England: Clarendon Press, 1921.

———. *Ten Thousand Buddhas*. London: B. Quaritch, Ltd., 1921.

Stephensen, Jessie. *From Old Stencils to Silk Screening*. New York: Charles Scribner's Sons, 1953.

Tuer, Andrew W. *Japanese Stencil Designs: One Hundred Outstanding Examples*. New York: Dover Publications, Inc., 1967. First published as *The Book of Delightful and Strange Designs Being One Hundred Facsimile Illustrations of the Japanese Stencil Cutter*. London: Leadenhall Press, 1892.

Vernon, R. *From Dark to Dawn in Fiji*. New York: F. H. Revell, 1890.

Waring, Janet. *Early American Stencils on Walls and Furniture*. New York: Dover Publications, Inc., 1968.

———. *Early American Wall Stencils, Their Origin, History, and Use*. New York: William R. Scott, 1942.

Index